William James Henderson

What is Good Music?

Suggestions to Persons Desiring to Cultivate a Taste in Musical Art. Third Edition

William James Henderson

What is Good Music?
Suggestions to Persons Desiring to Cultivate a Taste in Musical Art. Third Edition

ISBN/EAN: 9783337084691

Printed in Europe, USA, Canada, Australia, Japan

Cover: Foto ©Thomas Meinert / pixelio.de

More available books at **www.hansebooks.com**

WHAT IS GOOD MUSIC?

SUGGESTIONS TO PERSONS DESIRING
TO CULTIVATE A TASTE IN
MUSICAL ART

BY

W. J. HENDERSON

*Author of "The Story of Music," "Preludes and
Studies," etc.*

THIRD EDITION

NEW YORK
CHARLES SCRIBNER'S SONS
1899

TO
PHILIP HALE

CONTENTS

Prelude

Music and the other arts—Criticism as opposed to enjoyment—Influence of romanticism—Wagner and his theories—Phrases, sections, and melodies—Growth of the desire to understand music—Living with good music—Condition of the uninstructed listener—Hearing in the conventional way—Sonatas *versus* fandangoes—Hearing Bach's "Passion"—Chamber music as a soporific—Friends in need but not in deed. . . . . . . *Page* 3 — PRELUDE.

PART I.—THE QUALITIES OF GOOD MUSIC

THE ESSENTIALS OF FORM

Rhythm, Melody, and Harmony

Excellence of musical ideas—Musical high thinking—Laws which are recognizable—Musical form and history—Why needful to know form?—Music exists when heard—Necessity of repetition—Distribution of repetitions—Diversity in unity—Importance of separate functions—High grades of organization—Nature of rhythm—Elementary — CHAP. I.

Contents

CHAP. I.
rhythms—Simple and compound rhythms—Nature of melody—Nature of harmony—Melody and rhythm associated—Analyzing a common melody—The closing cadence—Explanation of phrases—Repetition of a motive—Satisfying the ear—Musical and poetic rhythms—Complexity of organization. . . . . , *Page* 13

Polyphonic Forms

CHAP. II.
Polyphonic system of repetition—The monophonic system—The harmonic basis—A tune accompanying itself—A tune accompanied by chords—Polyphonic music defined—Meaning of counterpoint—The fugue defined—Subject and answer—Counter-subject and stretto—What to listen for—The fugue's intellectuality—Age of polyphony—Lasso and Palestrina—Music originally formless—Beginning of song—Appearance of rhythm—Rhythm taken from text—The ecclesiastical chant—Obviousness of melodic form—The instrumental development—The fugues of J. S. Bach—Characteristics of polyphony—Mastery of rigid material. . . . . *Page* 27

Monophonic Forms

CHAP. III.
The solo-voice style—Dominance of song-thought—The sonata its issue—Period and stanza—Many schemes of repetition—The Rondo form—A Rondo in verse—Development of Rondo forms—The late Rondo form—The First Movement form—The slow introduction—Sometimes made important—The two chief themes—Relation of keys—Subjects and their relations—Use of episodes—Value of the "repeat"—The "working-out" part—Thematic development—Alterations of the subject—Altering the melody—Treatment and coloring—Difference in styles—Value of working out—Climax of a movement—The skeleton concealed—Essentials of sonata form—Vocal and instrumen-

Contents

CHAP. III.

tal styles—The second movement—The minuet with development—The minuet and scherzo—Origin of the scherzo—Scherzi by Bach—The true Beethoven scherzo—Form of the scherzo—Finale of the sonata—Modern innovations—The concerto form—Sonata the classic form—The era of musical beauty—The term "classical"—Absence of deep emotion—Beauty and the Sonata. . . . *Page* 41

Romantic Forms

CHAP. IV.

Recapitulation—The two great impulses—Classicism and Romanticism—Demand for expression—Beethoven's romanticism—Its effect on form—Community of theme—Schumann's fourth symphony — Its plan of development — The Symphonic poem—The programme overture—Liszt's piano concertos—Traits of romantic music. . . *Page* 63

Fundamental Principles

CHAP. V.

Balance and design—Essentials of form—Common to all music—Small *versus* large forms. . . . . *Page* 70

VOCAL FORMS

Church Counterpoint

CHAP. VI.

Mediæval church music—Essentials of vocal counterpoint—Beauty of church polyphony. . . . . *Page* 73

Simple Song Forms

CHAP. VII.

Age of the song—Song form and poetry—The cyclical song—Meaning in accompaniment—Value of form and style—Dramatic songs—Essentials of a good song—Variety of song forms. . . . . *Page* 75

Contents

Operatic Forms

CHAP. VIII.
Origin of opera—Monotony of recitative—Advent of the aria—Reign of vocal display—Tickling the ear—Abolishing set forms—Purpose of opera music—Fidelity to the text — Music as an expression — Kinds of recitative— "Recitative secco"—The arioso style—The aria da capo—Different kinds of aria—Artistic level of opera—Absolute music higher. . . . . *Page* 79

THE CONTENT OF MUSIC

The Sensuous

CHAP. IX.
Form not everything—Criticism of form and style—Fundamental qualities of music—Form implies content—Three fundamental forces—The sensuous element—Purely sensuous music—Sensuousness of the orchestra—Pleasure of the thoughtless—Factors of the sensuous—Composition and painting—Tone-color and art—The Sensuous a means—Color and Outline. . . . . *Page* 88

The Intellectual

CHAP. X.
"Music of the intellect"—Intellect and method—The Intellectual and design—Demands of musical design—A correct emotional scheme—Attributes of an organism—Organism in music—Hanslick on form—The Intellectual in history—Beethoven and the Intellectual—Music's highest organism. . . . . *Page* 97

The Emotional

CHAP. XI.
Music arouses emotion—Mistakes about musical emotion—Primary law of expression—Music imitates speech—

Contents

Power of musical expression—Limit of this expression—Music expresses moods—Not an indefinite expression—Errors of the hearer—Groundless expectations—What one may expect—Beethoven's emotional utterance—Evils of bad criticism—How not to criticise—Music wrongly censured—Conventions of expression—Descriptive music—Programme music—Telling a story—Value of opera music—Communication of emotion. . . . . *Page* 104

CHAP. XI.

Æsthetics of Music

What is the beautiful?—Kant on Beauty—Free and adherent beauty—Their place in music—Art and symbolism—Beauty and education—Art and judgment—Value of the Inevitable—Suitability of style—Fitness in opera music—Æsthetics of the emotional—Music and abstract Beauty—Form absolutely essential—Summary of musical beauty. . . . . *Page* 117

CHAP. XII.

PART II.—THE PERFORMANCE OF MUSIC

INSTRUMENTAL PERFORMANCE

The Orchestra

Performance a sure ground—Questions of fact—The modern orchestra—Its scope and power—Its three groups—The various instruments—Functions of the three choirs—The wood wind—Its minor groups—Its compass and variety—Close and dispersed writing—The brass choir—French horn passages—Trumpets and trombones—Use of kettle drums—The string quintet—Special effects—Muted

CHAP. XIII.

Chap. XIII.	strings—Relations of stringed instruments—The viola's character—Its dramatic power—The violoncello—Variety in the strings—Good orchestration—Solidity and balance —Contrast and variety—Hearing all the instruments— Good orchestral playing—Balance of tone—Smoothness of tone—Solidity of tone—Precision and unanimity— Light and shade—The middle voices—Duties of a conductor. . . . . *Page* 129

Chamber Music

Chap. XIV.	Homogeneity of tone—The pervasive " soloist "—Place of the piano—Beauty of quartet playing—Taste for chamber-music. . . . . , *Page* 151

The Piano

Chap. XV.	Ignorance about piano playing—Technic and tone-color—Music must be heard—Power of the interpreter— Paderewski an example—Object of piano technic—Emanuel Bach and Mozart—Clementi's style—Liszt, Chopin, and tone-color—Independence of fingers—The singing tone— Touch and pedalling—Rhythm and phrasing—Musical temperament — Emotion and performance — Control of emotion—Intellect in command—Province of the intellect —Emotion and shading — Historical justice — Making a reading—Analysis of the design—Adjustment of effects— Grasp of organic unity—Value of emotional power—Summary of the matter. . . . . *Page* 155

The Violin

Chap. XVI.	The violin technic—Accuracy of stopping—Quality of tone—Touch in bowing—Purity and sonority—Large and small tone—The bow arm—Special effects—Violins as singers—Intimacy of the violin. . . . . . *Page* 172

Contents

VOCAL PERFORMANCE

The Work of a Chorus

Requirements of choral singing—Orchestra and chorus—Balance of tone—Singing in tune—Importance of phrasing—Phrasing and the text—Light and shade—Refinement and size. . . . . *Page* 180

CHAP. XVII.

Solo Singing

Ignorance about singing—Temperament and agility—Highest type of singing—Voice and art—Difference of methods—Registers and equalization—Good tone-production—Clearness and freedom—Secret of attack—The legato style—Messa di voce—Vocalization—Distinct enunciation—Good phrasing—Regulation of breathing—Technic and art—Mme. Patti's skill—Ultimate purpose of song. . . . . *Page* 186

CHAP. XVIII.

INDEX. . . . . *Page* 199

What Is Good Music?

Prelude

THE right to like or dislike a musical composition without giving a reason has long been regarded as coexistent with human freedom. Music has been a sort of Cinderella of the arts, casually observed, incidentally admired, but generally treated as of no serious importance in the presence of her favored sisters, painting and poetry. No one presumed to pronounce an opinion on the merit of a picture or a statue who had not at least learned the difference between a pen-and-ink drawing and a water-color, and few persons would have ventured to write down Shakespeare an ass before having acquired a sufficient knowledge of poetry to tell a sonnet from a five-act tragedy. But it was deemed altogether fitting and, indeed, intellectually satisfying that Beethoven should be smugly patted on the back, Brahms viewed with

Music and the other arts.

What Is Good Music?

Prelude.

lifted brows, and Wagner convicted of lunacy by persons who could not, while in the concert-room, detect a fantasia masquerading as an overture, nor a suite disguised as a symphony—nay, more, who could not tell when the composer dropped the elementary rhythm of the valse to take up that of the polonaise. For music was, if you please, not matter to be reasoned about, but just to be listened to and to be enjoyed. "Who are these fellows," said the concert-goers, "with their prosy platitudes about music and her dignity as an art? Do we go into the concert-room to search for the skeleton under the beautiful flesh? Nay, let us feast our hearts upon the ravishing beauty of naked Sound, and let these anatomists go fall upon their own scalpels."

Criticism as opposed to enjoyment.

But even as they spoke there arose a race of composers who used the scalpel on their own art, and who cried aloud in the market-places for intellectual consideration. And these composers were forthwith discovered to be romanticists, who declared that music was not only beautiful, but throbbing with the pent-

Influence of romanticism.

Prelude

up passion of humanity. In her these found the elemental voice of mankind, the speech of fundamental emotions, the irresistible declaration of the primeval barbarian grandeur of the man and woman at gaze one upon the other; and they called the world to witness that when they sat down to compose music they were engaged in graving with subtler tools what the painter splashed with his brush and the poet traced with his pen.

Finally, one of these romanticists, a mad, uncontrollable fellow, whose convictions burnt into his soul with such fierce fire that they sent him running through the highways of the world screaming his agony into the faces of men, proclaimed his belief in a hybrid, acephalous thing called the art-work of the future, in which poetry, painting, acting, and music should unite and form an æsthetic Dagon to be worshipped in Gath and Askalon, and all the cities of the Philistines. And then the listeners to music said to one another, "Wherein do the works of this Utopian differ from those of Mozart and the prophets? We

Prelude.

Wagner and his theories.

Prelude.

Phrases, sections and melodies.

Growth of the desire to understand music.

hear a great confusion of sounds, but the aria and the trio and the finale are not." So they learned that there was a something called a *leit motif*, and that sometimes it was only a phrase, sometimes a section, and again a complete melody. Whereupon they became aware that they themselves did not know how a phrase, a section, or a complete melody might differ one from the other. And so, as has frequently happened since the beginning of the world, the woman timorously tasted the fruit of the tree of knowledge, and finding that it was good for food and to make one wise, " gave also unto her husband with her, and he did eat. And the eyes of them both were opened, and they knew that they were naked."

Assuredly, whatever may have been the course of musical culture in other lands, in the United States the appetite for an understanding of music was aroused by Wagner. Now many who have for years been sitting in the temples of the divine art in sloth and carelessness are crying out, "What shall I do to be saved?" It has been the happy expe-

Prelude

rience of the writer to meet with hundreds who were searching anxiously for the path that leads to musical salvation. Fortunately, it is not only a straight path, but a broad and short one. The person who desires to cultivate a discriminating taste in music may acquire the fundamental knowledge in a few short months. After that, one needs only to live much in an atmosphere of good music until the acquired principles become unconsciously the moving factors underlying all attention to the art. If, therefore, I venture to offer a few hints to those who find pleasure in listening to music, but desire to make that pleasure dependent not on fancy but on judgment, I may hope that not every man will deem me an impertinent fellow.

Let us suppose, then, forbearing reader, that you are in the state of the average music-lover. You get great enjoyment out of the opera, though you freely admit that you begin to be weary at the point where the inner brotherhood pricks up its ears and looks very wise. You attend the functions of the Boston Symphony Orchestra and the Phil-

marginalia:
PRELUDE.

Living with good music.

Condition of the uninstructed listener.

What Is Good Music?

PRELUDE.

Hearing in the conventional way.

harmonic Society, and when they play Haydn's works, you are quite content. You like also some of the symphonies of Mozart, some of Mendelssohn's, and parts of Beethoven's. But you are troubled by that dark-blue music of Tschaikowsky, and those impolite compositions of Dvořák; and you deem it an unpardonable rudeness on the part of any orchestra to confuse you with those tonal riddles of Brahms. Privately you are willing to admit that the slow movements of nearly all symphonies are as poppy and mandragora to you; and you surreptitiously go to the Sunday-evening concerts where the ballet-music of Massenet and Delibes refreshes your intellect by its appeal to your feet. You go to piano recitals when the buzz of public talk about the pianist excites your curiosity, but you do wish the artist would let those dreary Beethoven sonatas, Schumann fantasias, and Bach fugues rest, and stick to his Chopin valses, Rubinstein barcarolles, and Liszt fandangoes.

Sonatas versus fandangoes.

As for the oratorio, you, like others, go religiously once a year to hear the sounds with reference to their succession. No amount of rhythmic originality would satisfy the ear if a single tone were maintained throughout. In order to have melody, we must have movement from lower tones to higher, or *vice versa*. The melodic succession, therefore, is dependent upon changes of pitch. It is a succession of tones of different elevation. The third element of form—harmony—is the distribution of sounds with reference to their union. It is the science of arranging the effect of tones which are to be heard simultaneously, and it also governs the sequences of the groups, or chords, as they are called. Our modern music is so thoroughly founded on harmony that it is difficult to conceive of any familiar air as dissociated from its usual chord arrangement. A new harmonization gives the air apparently a new melody. For example:

Nature of melody.

Nature of harmony.

The Essentials of Form

Chap. I.

Melody and rhythm associated.

It is equally true that melody is indissolubly associated with rhythm, and that an alteration of the rhythm will give a new character to a melodic succession, thus:

We may lay harmonic form aside for the present and confine ourselves to the study of melodic form. The simplest and most intelligible method of procedure is to take a common tune and pull it apart to see how it is built:

Analyzing a common melody.

This is the first part of the principal theme in the opening movement of Beethoven's Seventh Symphony. An examination will show that it divides itself into two equal parts of four measures each, the first part, which may be called the proposition, ending at the point marked by an arrow. Long habit has taught the human ear that a melody is not ended till it closes with a cadence returning it to the tonic key; hence on hearing the suspension at the arrow we realize that the sense is incomplete, just as we would if we heard a man say, "If I go down town to-morrow," and then pause. But when the man adds, "I shall buy new shoes," he completes the sense and the sentence. Just so Beethoven completes his sentence by adding the second half, or conclusion. These two equal parts of a melody are called sections, and the portion making complete sense, whether composed of two or more sections, is called a period.

A further examination will show that each section is naturally divided into two balancing parts of two measures each, and that each of these parts has a perfectly defined shape and motion and a point of repose, or partial repose. These parts are called phrases. The germ of the phrase is the motive, which

The closing cadence.

Explanation of phrases.

indeed is the germ of the whole melody. It defines the rhythm and sets the figure for the melody. In the example quoted, the motive is coincident with the first phrase, but, of course, this is not always the case. In Beethoven's Fifth Symphony the motive is this:

while the first phrase is this:

Repetition of a motive.

From the example quoted above, the reader will be able to gather what was meant by the phrase "distribution of repetitions." He will note, for instance, that the repetition may be either rhythmic, or melodic, or both. The motive, announced in the first measure, is repeated exactly in both rhythm and melody in the fifth (the first measure of the second section). So, indeed, is the whole of the first phrase. The third measure of the first section is identical in rhythm, but not in melody, with the third measure of the second section. The change in melody is dictated by the composer's perception of the most suitable method of returning to the tonic. He could have used the third measure of the first section over, but it would have deprived him of the reposeful effect gained by the B preceding the final A, which requires a harmony passing from dominant to tonic, and thus giving a satisfying cadence. The fourth measure of the first section repeats the rhythm of the third measure with the lengths of the first two notes transposed for the obvious purpose of accentuating the suspension, and of satisfying a demand of harmony which need not be discussed here.

This examination of the first period of a melody by Beethoven reveals to us some of the principles of elementary form. It shows us that rhythms and metres in music are distributed in very much the same way as they are in poetry, and that the identity of a tune is established by the repetitions of the fundamental melodic ideas of which it is made. Any simple song—a folk-song, a ballad, or one of the ordinary opera airs—can be analyzed in the manner above employed and without difficulty.

Satisfying the ear.

Musical and poetic rhythms.

CHAP. I.

Complexity of organization.

But when we come to a composition in which several complete tunes are used, or in which even one is used with much variety of musical treatment, we find ourselves in the presence of one of those higher organizations in which the system of construction does not so readily make itself known. Yet it is not beyond the power of any listener to learn to perceive the formal construction of a composition to which he is listening, and in doing so to enjoy the beauty of its design or to detect fundamental weaknesses in it.

II

Polyphonic Forms

THE student of music will soon discover that there are two great classes of forms—polyphonic and monophonic—many-voiced and single-voiced. In the former he will find that the organism is effected by repeating (at a distance of one or more measures) in a second voice what has already been sung or played by a first. The complexity of this system of repetition may be made very great, as in a four-voiced canon, and the system is capable of marvellous detail and compactness, as in the fugue. The monophonic system, on the other hand, makes its repetitions within the limits of a single-voiced melody having a subsidiary accompaniment. Its simplest form is the song, and its highest the symphony. The student should endea-

Polyphonic system of repetition.

The monophonic system.

The Essentials of Form

CHAP. II.

vor to form a clear conception of the essential difference between polyphonic and monophonic writing. In the polyphonic style we are confronted by a melody repeated at different intervals by different voices, and forming its own harmonies. In the monophonic style, sometimes called the harmonic, we have a single-voiced melody whose succession of tones is conceived as an organic part of a succession of chords out of which the accompaniment is formed. Here is an example of polyphonic writing (a canon—of which a definition will be given later) which will show the reader how a tune is made to work as its own accompaniment:

The harmonic basis.

The reader will note that in the second measure the first voice begins, at an interval half a tone higher, the tune begun by the second voice in the first measure. The first voice follows the second in intoning the air, always just a measure behind and half a tone higher; and the tune working against itself in this way provides its own harmonies. This is a fair illustration of the process of polyphonic construction, while a brief quotation from the "Tannhäuser" overture will suffice to illustrate the nature of the monophonic style and its harmonic character:

A tune accompanying itself.

Here it is obvious that the lower voices do not repeat the melody of the upper voice, nor are they essentially melodious in themselves, as they would have to be in polyphonic writing. The upper voice —the melody—is, however, plainly conceived as an inseparable part of a succession of chords which not only form its accompaniment, but add distinctive

A tune accompanied by chords.

features to its character. The reader ought now to be prepared to accept certain definitions which bear upon form.

Polyphonic music defined.
Polyphonic music is that in which several voices, each intoning a melody, move simultaneously without discord.

Meaning of counterpoint.
Polyphonic writing is based on counterpoint, which is the art of constructing two or more melodies which may proceed together with correct harmony. The different voices in a contrapuntal composition are not required to repeat the same melody. Two or more individual tunes may be heard at once. In the finale of Wagner's "Die Meistersinger" prelude five melodies are going simultaneously. When the same melody is repeated by the various voices, we have a canonic form, of which the highest development is the fugue. A canon, as I have shown, is a composition in which the voices begin one after another, each intoning precisely the same melody. The laws of canon require that the point of entry, having been established, must be followed by all the voices; that is, if the second voice begins one measure after the first, the

third must begin one measure after the second. Furthermore, the voices must rigidly preserve the first intervallic difference; that is, if the second voice takes up the tune a third above the first, it must follow out the melody at that interval. The reader will at once perceive that canonic writing requires profound mastery of musical material, and that it is likely to interest us more by the intellectual qualities displayed in its construction than by its merely sensuous charms. A fugue is a composition written in strict polyphonic style according to laws laid down by the elder masters. Bach is the accepted head of the school of fugue writers, and his works formulate the entire code of practice. It is quite unnecessary and foreign to the general purpose of this book to describe the entire construction of a fugue; but its general features ought to be pointed out. The required parts of a fugue are the Subject, the Answer, the Countersubject, and the Stretto.

The Subject is the theme, the fundamental melody. The Answer is the correlative of the Subject. The former is

The fugue defined.

Subject and answer.

usually the first phrase of the fugue, and the latter the second phrase, and the polyphonic character of the composition is at once revealed by the fact that the Answer is simply the Subject repeated at a different pitch, thus:

Countersubject and stretto.

The Countersubject is that part of the melody which is so constructed as to form the accompaniment to the Answer. The Stretto is a drawing together of the parts near the end of the fugue by causing their entries to overlap. The student will find that the Answer is sometimes an inversion of the Subject. Sometimes it repeats the Subject in longer notes (augmentation) and sometimes in shorter notes (diminution). Various other devices are employed to give life and interest to a fugue, but there is no necessity of dwelling upon them here.

Accurate and complete criticism of a fugue is only possible to one who is fully acquainted with the laws of fugue; but an intelligent estimate of the value of a fugal composition may be made by any person who knows the general principles of polyphony. The listener to a fugue should identify the Subject and watch for the Answer. He should note whether it is direct or inverted, or whether it has been augmented or diminished. At the same time he should hear the Countersubject and bear it in mind.

Thereafter he should follow the interweaving of these melodic parts and endeavor to decide whether it shows ingenuity or baldness, plasticity, or stiffness, power and fecundity, or unsuccessful effort and barrenness. Above all, the great question is: Does it make music? Is it beautiful within the field of polyphonic writing, or is it ugly? If it has balance, symmetry, clarity, and logical devclopment it will have the front of beauty. It will come with all the convincing force of a clear argument. The fugue is an intellectual product, and it must be studied with the intellect. He who listens for rhythm and melody only,

What to listen for.

The fugue's intellectuality.

will be disappointed in all fugues, even those of Bach. The proper endeavor is to follow the interweaving of the voice-parts and discover what ingenious and striking effects are produced by the workings of the different phrases of a melody against one another.

Age of Polyphony. Polyphonic writing is the oldest form of modern music, and the first few centuries of musical history were taken up with the labors of industrious and gifted musicians in developing this kind of music. The masters of the famous Netherlands school, which flourished in the fifteenth and sixteenth centuries, were most accomplished writers of polyphonic music, and originated most of its laws. Their music was all vocal and without accompaniment (*a capella*). It reached its highest development in the *Lasso and Palestrina.* compositions of Orlando Lasso, and the noble works of Palestrina owe their existence to the science formulated by the Netherlanders. The development of this church polyphony was an artificial process, yet it was inevitable that it should have preceded the monophonic, or harmonic style.

Polyphonic Forms

Music was originally a free dictation of fancy or feeling, and it dates back to the night of time. When I say "free," I mean in respect of form. It was probably a kind of intonation employed in the solemn speech of ceremonials, as instanced in the first book of Samuel, x. 5: "After that thou shalt come to the hill of God, where is the garrison of the Philistines: and it shall come to pass, when thou art come thither to the city, that thou shalt meet a company of prophets coming down from the high place, with a psaltery, and a tabret, and a pipe, and a harp, before them; and they shall prophesy." Further historical support of the probability that song began in mere inflections of the voice is found in the old Neume notation, which preceded the notation now in use. The Neumes were marks, somewhat like the Greek accents, placed over the vowels of a text, to indicate the intervals up or down through which the voice should pass in intoning. What we now recognize as melody was developed by gradual growth from intonations of this kind. Rhythm must have made its appearance

---

CHAP. II.

Music originally formless.

Beginning of song.

in music as soon as it did in the verses to which music was set. Eugene Veron, in his "Æsthetics," says:

Appearance of rhythm.

" A very important characteristic of ancient languages was rhythm. The more or less regular recurrence of intonations and of similar cadences constitutes for children and savages the most agreeable form of music. The more the rhythm is accentuated the better they are pleased; they love not only its sound, but its movement also. . . . The most civilized nations cannot escape this tyranny of rhythm. . . . Rhythm seems, indeed, to contain some general law, possessing power over almost all living things. One might say that rhythm is the dance of sound, as dancing is the rhythm of movement. The farther we go back into the past the more marked and dominant is it found in language. It is certain that at one period of the development of humanity rhythm constituted the only music known, and it was even intertwined with language itself."

Rhythm taken from text.

The earliest music, then, must have been a kind of intonation in which the rhythm was simply that of the text, and the melody a derivative of the inflections of the voice, as dictated by the natural utterance of that text. The most artificial attempts in music have been based on the idea that we could return to that primitive form. One attempt was that of the founders of the church chant; the other was that of the inventors of opera. It is incumbent upon us to consider now only the first of these. At the beginning of modern artistic music (not the music of the people, the folk-songs) we find the Gregorian chant, a musically formless droning of the church liturgy, in which the only rhythm was that of the text, and the melody was the outgrowth of mere intonation.

    The first cultivators of artistic music were the monks, who found as material ready to hand only the folk-songs of the people and the music of the Greeks. The latter appealed to these cloistered mediæval scholars as the only proper material for churchly use, and they set to work to develop a system. It was inevitable that modern scientific music should begin with the invention of the *materia musicæ*. These old monks had first to develop melody, and it was natural that having once started upon that labor they should carry it out to its logical issue. Melodic form is more obvious than harmonic, hence they developed it. Having once got the melodic idea firmly fixed in their minds, they conceived a composition to be a combination of melodies, and when at some period about the end of the eleventh century the device of imitating in a second voice the melody uttered by the first was invented, counterpoint, single and double, grew with great rapidity.

The polyphonic forms in music were developed in the interval between 1100 and the death of Bach, 1750. After Lasso and Palestrina, *a capella* church music went backward rather than forward, but polyphony continued to be developed by instrumental composers and found its issue in the North German fugue. Nothing has been added to the laws of fugue since Bach's day, and the difficulty of producing good fugues increases every year, because available subjects are slowly being exhausted. Those who desire to comprehend fully the scope and power of *a capella* church music should study the works of Lasso and Palestrina, while for perfection in the instrumental form they should devote their attention to Bach's fugues. In studying the polyphonic works one should recognize their

Polyphonic Forms

intellectual and emotional characteristics.

First, note the profundity of the musical learning. Contrapuntal writing is the most learned kind of composition, because every measure must be made in obedience to fixed laws. The polyphonic period began with the discovery of these laws, and the early composers exhausted their ingenuity in the invention of canons by inversion, by augmentation and diminution, by retrogression, etc. The constant study of such forms led to the second feature of their work, which must be noted, *viz.*, mastery of musical material. In spite of the rigid requirements of the polyphonic laws these composers gradually acquired a power to make seemingly inflexible forms do their bidding. This power is manifested in its highest degree in the apparently spontaneous flexibility of the works of Lasso, Palestrina, and Bach. The third feature to be noted is the serenity of the emotional atmosphere of these works. The earliest polyphonic writers displayed no feeling at all. Their only effort was to be as ingenious as possible. And in the

Characteristics of polyphony.

Mastery of rigid material.

culmination of the *a capella* school one can find only a pure, chaste, and gentle religious feeling. One seeks in vain for the note of dramatic passion, which found its way into artistic music after the birth of opera and the adoption of the melodic style of the folk-song.

III

Monophonic Forms

THE essential difference between polyphonic and monophonic form lies in the distribution of the repetitions. In the former the idea is repeated by several voices working harmoniously. In the latter it is repeated by one voice. In the former a tune is made to act as its own accompaniment, and the system is designed wholly to enable repetitions of thematic ideas to be made as accompaniments to one another. In the monophonic style the song-thought prevails; the single-voiced melody is sung to a subordinate accompaniment, and the system of repetitions is designed so that the melodic ideas are presented symmetrically by the one voice. Polyphonic devices are sometimes introduced in monophonic compositions for the sake of contrast and

The solo-voice style.

Dominance of song-thought.

The Essentials of Form

The sonata its issue.

variety, but the monophonic part of the work clings to its own system of repetitions. The history of the development of the monophonic style is very interesting, but it cannot be introduced in this volume. The reader can find accounts of it in most histories of music, or in Dr. Parry's admirable "Evolution of the Art of Music." The sonatas and symphonies of Haydn, Mozart, Beethoven, and their successors, the great overtures and the famous concertos are all written in the monophonic style, and nearly all of them are in the sonata form, which is the highest organization of monophonic repetitions. The elements of the song form, which lies at the basis of the sonata and kindred modern forms, have already been set forth. They are the elements of all melodies.

Period and stanza.

The period, which has already been described, may be regarded as the musical equivalent of the stanza in poetry. Let us see how this is.

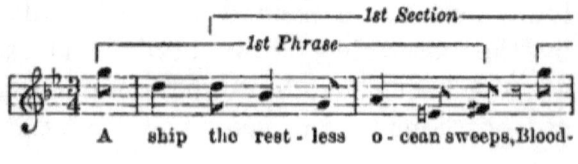

Monophonic Forms

Here is a period of Senta's ballad in "The Flying Dutchman," with the English text. It becomes plain at a glance that each phrase of the music is the equivalent of a line of poetry, that a section equals half a stanza, and that the period is equal to the stanza in extent and rhythmic construction. Now, as it is possible to construct many varieties of poetic stanza, so it is possible to construct many varieties of period, and hence there is a wide field open to the musician at the very outset of his arrangement of repetitions. Musical rhythms are capable of much greater extension than poetic rhythms, so that the composer may construct musical stanzas much more flexible than the stanzas of the poet. The necessity of repetition of the

Many schemes of repetition.

Chap. III.

The Rondo form.

principal musical idea led the earlier composers to the establishment of the Rondo form, upon which many subsequent developments were based. The Rondo is a "round." Its construction is cyclical, its chief characteristic being regular returns to the first subject. The Rondo in music is similar to the French poetic form called Rondeau, which is a short poem so arranged that the opening and closing two lines are the same. Some variations of the form, which approach more nearly the musical form, have the two lines also repeated in the middle. An excellent example is the following charming poem by the late H. C. Bunner:

A Rondo in verse.

" O honey of Hymettus Hill,
　　Gold brown and cloying sweet to taste,
　Wert here for the soft amorous bill
　　Of Aphrodite's courser placed?

" Thy musky scent what virginal chaste
　　Blossom was ravished to distil,
　O honey of Hymettus Hill,
　　Gold brown and cloying sweet to taste?

" What upturned calyx drank its fill
　　When ran the draught divine to waste,

That her white hands were doomed to fill—
  Sweet Hebe fallen and disgraced—
O honey of Hymettus Hill,
  Gold brown and cloying sweet to taste?"

The reader will note how naturally the first two lines recur. This is one of the features of the art-Rondo in music. In its earliest state it began with a subject (a melody) of one or two periods. The composition then wandered through several keys and introduced considerable mere passage-work, after which it returned to the principal subject. Later composers introduced a second subject, and still later ones a third, but the first was always repeated after each of them. The first of these rondo forms — that with one subject—was in use by composers from François Couperin (organist and clavier player, Paris, 1688–1733) to Haydn. The second and third forms were those of Mozart and Beethoven. Students of the latter master will find a good example of the second form in the sonata in A, opus 2, No. 2. The fully developed third form is as follows: first subject, second subject in the dominant key, first subject, third sub-

Chap. III.

Development of Rondo forms.

The late Rondo form.

ject, first subject, second subject in the tonic, coda.

The fundamental difference between the Rondo and the First Movement form, which is the distinguishing part of the modern Sonata, is in the middle portion. In the Rondo there is a simple statement of themes connected by more or less relevant matter. In the First Movement form, or Sonata form, as it is frequently called, after the statement of the first and second themes, there follows a middle part devoted to a musical elaboration of these themes—a working-out, as it is called—after which the themes are restated, and the movement is brought to a conclusion. The three parts of the Sonata form, then, may be designated Proposition, Discussion, and Conclusion.

First movements usually begin with a slow introduction, and concert-goers will find them indicated on programmes in some such way as this: "Adagio—allegro con brio." The adagio here is the slow introduction. Sometimes this is omitted, as in the "Eroica" symphony, in which the statement of the first theme of the movement proper is prefaced only by two staccato chords. On the other hand, the introduction is sometimes developed to an important extent, as in Beethoven's Seventh Symphony. The slow introduction may foreshadow what is to come, and so add to the general coherence of the movement. The allegro itself must contain two principal subjects, varied and contrasted in style and in a symphony so made as to give opportunity for changes of instrumental coloring.

Sometimes made important.

The existence of the two contrasted themes is a *sine qua non* of modern sonata writing. In the earliest sonatas the first movement had only one theme, and as a result the development was limited. In the later sonatas the principle of contrast became more and more fully established, until now it is accepted that the first theme is to be vigorous, or, at least, animated, and the second fluent and melodious. Many writers speak of the second as the cantabile theme. The first subject may be brief or it may be a melody of several periods in the song form. But the studious

The two chief themes.

Relation of keys.

Subjects and their relations.

listener will find that the germinal part of the first subject is usually a strong and clearly defined motive, constructed with an especial view to its possibilities of development in the working-out portion of the movement. Contrast between the two subjects is increased by change of key. The first subject is always in the key of the symphony. When that key is well established, the composer prepares the way for a change of tonality. The old-fashioned way was to lead up to a suspension and then pass to the second subject in the dominant.* For instance, in a symphony in C the writer would lead up to a chord in D, and so modulate to his second subject

---

* For the benefit of the reader who has not studied harmony, it may be briefly noted that the key in which a composition stands is called the tonic, the fifth tone above that the dominant, and the fourth the subdominant. Thus in the key of C, G is the dominant, and F the subdominant. A minor is the relative minor of C. Immediately related keys are those which may be reached by direct diatonic modulations, as E minor, E major, or A-flat major. Foreign keys are those which can be reached only by passing through several other keys, or by chromatic modulation, as F-sharp, C-sharp minor, B-flat minor.

Monophonic Forms

in G. If the sonata began in a minor key, the second subject was in the relative major. The later writers, however, have advanced much beyond the old rules, and second subjects are written now in almost any immediately related key. Uncertainty of tonality is avoided by not using foreign keys in the propositional * part of the symphony. After the principal subjects are stated, there may be introduced one or two subsidiary or episodal subjects, and thus we come to the end of the first part. It is worthy of note that some of the contemporaneous composers show a tendency to advance the episodal subject to the importance of a third principal theme; but it is still kept in subordination to the other two. At the end of the part of the movement containing the announcement of the subjects, the older composers always wrote a double bar and a repeat. The repeat is now sometimes omitted by composers, but

Use of episodes.

Value of the "repeat."

---

* I use this word in one of its pure classical Latin senses. Propositio—a principal subject, a theme. Cicero, "De Oratoria," 3.

seldom with good effect. It is better that the subject-matter of a movement should be heard twice, in order that it may be firmly fixed in the mind of the hearer.

After the repeat comes the expository part of the movement, called the free fantasia or working out. It has already been called in this volume the discussion. In this part the composer gives his imagination free reign, and may employ all the devices of music in discussing or working out the themes previously stated. It is obvious that to produce a well-knit structure he must stick to his texts and not allow extraneous or disconnected matter to creep in. Yet he may very properly employ that form of thematic development which consists in the evolution of new matter directly from the old. It is indispensable, of course, that the direct relation of the new matter to the old should be readily discernible. Thematic development in its various forms is the highest type of working out. Its means are many, but it will be sufficient for the purposes of the present work to quote the following from Ernst

Monophonic Forms

Pauer's excellent primer on "Musical Forms:"

(1.) "The motive or principal subject is transformed rhythmically, whilst its harmony and melody remain undisturbed; in other words, the value of the notes is altered, the notes are multiplied or diminished, long notes are compressed into short ones, short ones expanded into long, the accentuation is altered, rhythmical changes, syncope, anticipations, etc., are introduced, the time is transformed from common into triple, and the speed is altered by retardation or acceleration."

(2.) "Melodious alteration with unaltered harmony and rhythm, partial variations of the members constituting the melody, application of changes of direct movement into counter-movement, and *vice versa;* elaboration and ornamentation of parts of the principal melody," etc.

(3.) "Alteration of harmony and melody, the rhythm being left intact; by the rhythm in this case is maintained the only resemblance with the principal motive."

(4.) "Alteration of the harmony; application of different successions of chords; transposition from major into minor key, and *vice versa*, which, of course, also affects the nature of the melody."

(5.) "Alteration of melody and rhythm; thus the thematic resemblance with the principal motive is vested in the harmony, which, of course, must consist of a very strongly pronounced and characteristic succession of chords."

(6.) "Alteration of the accompaniment; altera-

The Essentials of Form

Chap. III.

Treatment and coloring.

Difference in styles.

tion of a polyphonic style into a more simple one, and the reverse; variation of the supplementary accompanying parts in a characteristic manner."

(7.) "Variety of the contrapuntal treatment; imitative and canonic treatment; transposition of the motive into other parts; inversion by means of double counterpoint."

(8.) "Alteration of force and coloring of sound" (by dynamic or instrumental effects).

(9.) "Alteration of register" (changing pitch of melody).

(10.) "Alteration of expression with regard to legato, staccato, portamento," etc.

Only the first five of these means belong strictly to what is called thematic development. In the other five there is no development of a theme, but merely changes in its presentation. The first five, therefore, are of a higher order than the second five. The second five are found more frequently in symphonies than in sonatas for solo instruments, because the instrumental combinations in the orchestra render them easy of production. In regard to the value of the working out of themes I take pleasure in quoting further from Mr. Pauer, because what he says bears not only upon the

Monophonic Forms

First Movement form, but upon all highly organized music. He says:

> "The listener experiences a feeling of satisfaction as the order, system, gradual appearance and disappearance of a melody, harmony, or rhythm will be for him an object of curiosity, interest, and gratification. Thematic work is a musical maxim that is based on the laws of nature herself; it is identical with the law of organic production. This law demands that every product of the animal or vegetable world must develop itself according to a fixed economic order and the nature of the germ contained within it. The instrumental works of Haydn, Mozart, Beethoven, and others of our best composers, display a thoroughly logical and systematic development, which gradually unfolds itself from the germ or first idea to the point we technically call the climax."

The hearer will usually find the climax of a movement built on the first movement form in the working-out part, though it is sometimes reserved for the coda. After the working-out comes the recapitulation, or conclusion, in which both principal subjects are restated in the tonic key. The coda (tail-piece) brings the movement to an end. A simple outline of the First Movement form is this:

Marginal notes: CHAP. III. — Value of working out. — Climax of a movement.

The Essentials of Form

CHAP. III.

First Part, Proposition.	Second Part, Discussion.	Third Part, Conclusion.
Slow introduction. First subject, animated, tonic key. Second subject, cantabile, relative key. Episodes. Repeat.	Thematic development of first and second subjects: Free fantasia unrestricted in form.	First subject, tonic key. Second subject, tonic key. Coda.

The skeleton concealed.

The music-lover will bear in mind that this is a skeleton, and that in the living work he will find it covered with the flesh of beauty. It will not appear in its naked articulations, as I have set them forth with Mr. Pauer's aid; but it will determine the form of the composition just as the human skeleton determines the form of man. You will never mistake the body for the limbs of a well-made composition simply because you cannot see the framework.

Essentials of sonata form.

So much for what is called the First Movement, or Sonata form. It has been described separately because it embodies the essentials of cyclic form, the variety of form in which the masterpieces of absolute music are generally cast. The reader will note that its essentials are its tripartite form, its contrast of thematic material, its development of that mate-

Monophonic Forms

rial, and its return to the original proposition. In all high classes of music, contrast and development of themes will be found. The simple proposition of a melody belongs primarily to the realm of song; the discussion of a melodic subject is specifically the privilege of absolute instrumental music. The song form in an extended variety is often transferred to instrumental music, and is frequently found in symphonic slow movements.

The second movement of a symphony is usually a slow one, and is variable in form. It sometimes closely resembles the First Movement form, the working-out portion being much curtailed or altogether omitted. For an example, see the slow movement of Beethoven's sonata, opus 31, No. 2. Sometimes the rondo form is employed, as in Beethoven's "Sonata Pathetique," and in other cases the theme and variations are used. It is not necessary to explain a theme and variations, but it is worthy of note that Beethoven sometimes separates successive variations by passages built out of the material at hand. Another form of

Chap. III.

Vocal and Instrumental styles.

The second movement.

CHAP. III.

The minuet with development.

The minuet and scherzo.

slow movement is that sometimes called the cavatina. It consists of a long passage in song form, followed by an instrumental recitative, and a return to the original melody. The most familiar example of it is the slow movement of Chopin's F minor piano concerto.

The third movement is a minuet or a scherzo. The minuet is a movement in a dance rhythm of French origin. It is in three-fourth time and was originally played slowly. A second melody was added in early times, and as this was always written in three-part harmony, it was called the trio. The form is extremely simple in the earlier works, being simply

MINUET.	Development.	Modulation with close in tonic.
	Chief Subject.	Tonic.
TRIO.	Development.	Modulation with close in tonic of trio.
	Chief Subject.	Relative major or minor.
MINUET.	Development.	Modulation with close in tonic.
	Chief Subject.	Tonic key.

Monophonic Forms

a plain proposition of the minuet melody, the trio, and a return to the minuet. A more ambitious style led to a form something like that of the first movement. Its outline is shown in the table opposite.

Haydn once said, "Oh, that some one would teach us how to write a new minuet!" Beethoven gratified the desire of the father of the symphony when he introduced the scherzo. The word is Italian, and means joke or jest. The term was first used as a direction to players, when it appeared as scherzando. But in the early part of the seventeenth century Italian canzonets were popular in Germany and were called *scherzi musicali*. When it became the custom to name the different parts of a musical composition, the terms *allegretto scherzando* and *presto scherzando* appeared. We find several instances in the sonatas of Emanuel Bach, and even Johann Bach wrote a scherzo in one of his suites. The modern scherzo is a development of the minuet. Haydn took the stateliness out of the minuet by increasing its speed and introducing the element of humor ; but

Chap. III.

Origin of the scherzo.

Scherzi by Bach.

CHAP. III.

The true Beethoven scherzo.

Form of the scherzo.

the transition to the scherzo was definitely made by Beethoven, though he did not abandon the minuet, which appears in many of his works. The difference between the minuet and the scherzo is one of feeling rather than of form. The time is quicker, the rhythm is more varied and the working out is frequently much more elaborate. But it is the character of the music that makes a scherzo. Rollicking gayety as in that of the Seventh Symphony, grim mystery as in that of the Fifth, and even tragic portent as in that of the Ninth were introduced by Beethoven, and composers of to-day often transform the scherzo into a wild orgy as Tschaikowsky has done in some of his symphonies, while Dvořák has even substituted for it the "furiant," whose title is self-explanatory. The form of the scherzo is precisely the same as that of the minuet. This is an excellent demonstration of the plasticity of the classic forms. The content of the movement has changed completely, but its outward shape remains the same. The trio continues to supply the necessary contrast, the point of repose, without which so

Monophonic Forms

vivacious a movement would inevitably become wearisome.

The last movement of a sonata or symphony is generally an allegro. In the earlier classic compositions it was the custom to make this movement lighter and more genial than the first. This custom did not survive, however, and in recent symphonies the final movement is often the most ambitious. The last movement is often written in the same form as the first, except that the repeat of the first part is generally omitted and the working-out is not made so elaborate. The Rondo form is often employed, and occasionally the theme and variations. Modern writers often depart widely from the classic form of the sonata, as, for instance, in the case of Tschaikowsky's "Symphonie Pathétique," which has the slow movement last and the working out of each theme of the first movement immediately after the announcement of the theme. But the old form is easily recognizable as the foundation of all that has followed it, and it was bound to be so because it was the fullest embodiment of the

Chap. III.

Finale of the sonata.

Modern innovations.

fundamental principles of form in music.

The concerto form.

I have spoken of sonata and symphony, but the concerto is also in the sonata form. The purpose of the concerto is to display the resources of some solo instrument, and it is usually written in three movements, allegro, adagio, and allegro. The scherzo is omitted in this three-movement form, but there are four-movement concertos containing the scherzo. The working-out parts of the first and last movements in concertos are not so elaborate as in symphonies, but are devoted rather to the exhibition of the powers of the solo instrument. It is customary to introduce near the close of the first movement a long cadenza for the soloist, and a few concertos have cadenzas also in their closing movements.

Sonata the classic form.

The sonata form was the form perfected and employed by the great classic masters of instrumental music. The classic era in music was that in which monophonic form reached its highest development, and all who desire to obtain an acquaintance with symmetrical construction in its finest revelations must look to the classic composers. In examining the intellectual and emotional characteristics of the classic era, we are convinced that this was the golden age of pure musical beauty. We find no thunder of tragedy, no paroxysm of passion in Haydn and Mozart, nor in the early works of Beethoven. The works of Beethoven's middle period are transitional. They are classic in form, but romantic in spirit. His later works belong altogether to the romantic period. Hence we are justified in noting as the first of the characteristics of the classic era symmetry of form. So important an element was formal beauty that, even at the present time, works which follow closely the classic forms are said to belong to the classical school, though nothing can be regarded strictly as classic which has not endured the test of time.

A second distinctive characteristic of the era was the subordination of profound musical learning to a pleasing style. One has only to remember the geniality of the music of Haydn, Mo-

Chap. III.

The era of musical beauty.

The term "classical."

zart, and the early Beethoven, the simple and tuneful subjects, the bright, good-natured, and perspicuous treatment, to understand what is meant by this subordination. A natural concomitant of such a style was the serenity and sweetness of the emotional atmosphere of the music. Haydn thought that to be a great composer was to write with "good taste." Rubinstein, with much reason, called Mozart "eternal sunshine in music." In short, the classic era was the period of pure musical beauty, and the secrets of that beauty are to be sought most successfully by an examination into the methods of design employed by the masters of the period. The sonata was the representative work of the time, and a knowledge of the sonata form is an absolute necessity to the understanding and enjoyment of compositions written in the classic style. It is also necessary to an appreciation of all absolute music of a later birth, and freer form, because the new forms are all developed from the sonata.

IV

Romantic Forms

WE have seen that the polyphonic period was devoted to the discovery of musical material and to the development of the purely melodic form, in which every voice-part was melodious. We have seen that the classical period was devoted to the exposition of pure beauty in music, and that it developed a complex yet symmetrical form, in which single-voiced melody based on harmonic chords was used. We now come to the romantic music, in which the older forms were modified to meet the demands of self-expression.

Throughout the history of music we find, constantly striving with one another, two impulses—classicism and romanticism. The terms are somewhat freely used, and frequently misunder-

Recapitulation.

The two great impulses.

Chap. IV.

Classicism and Romanticism.

Demand for expression.

stood. The uninformed person calls all good music classical, as distinguished from operetta or dance-music or popular songs. But by writers on music these terms are used, somewhat arbitrarily, to distinguish music in which pure beauty of form and matter is the prevailing feature from that in which the composer's fancy governs and makes the form. The former kind is called classical for reasons which have already been given; the latter is known as romantic. The contest between classicism and romanticism began very naturally as soon as musical science had formulated sufficient law to enable composers to work according to some system. A system being established, some impulse was necessary to urge an advance beyond its limitations. That impulse was found in the imperious demands of original minds for freer expression. Those demands were purely romantic, but they always led to the development of forms. Hence the growth of the classic period itself was due to the urgency of romanticism.

But this must be said: The perfecting of form is a purely intellectual process.

Romantic Forms

Hence the dominance of formal development was due to a belief that form was of paramount importance in music and to a determination to work according to that belief. The dominance of romanticism, or free emotional impulse, could come only when composers had arrived at the intellectual conviction that this impulse ought to be permitted to make its own forms according to its needs.

This conviction found its first emphatic expression among the classic writers when Beethoven introduced his pregnant modifications into the sonata form, joining the second and third movements of piano concertos, and making a continuous flow of the scherzo and the finale of the Fifth Symphony in order that his thought might not be hampered by established forms. In the freedom with which he distributed his keys, and in his invention of the scherzo, Beethoven, who was the culmination of the classic, and the foundation of the romantic, school, further showed how emotional impulse was to stretch the limits of form. Schubert's art-songs went side by side with Beethoven's symphonies in

Beethoven's romanticism.

Its effect on form.

preaching the gospel of freedom from formalism, and led the way to the forms of Schumann and Liszt.

Schumann's modifications of the symphonic form consisted in uniting all four movements in one continuous flow, as in his D minor symphony, and in the employment of the device which has been called "partial community of theme." By this is meant the transfer of certain thematic ideas from one movement to another. In some modern compositions melodic subjects announced in the first movement appear with unexpected persistency in other movements, sometimes subjected to developing processes and at other times maintaining the identity of a fixed idea. In his D minor symphony, Schumann prescribed that the four movements should be in "one piece"—that is, played through without a break. The community of theme is worked out in this composition with a thoroughness which has not been excelled by any later composer. The motive of the introduction of the first movement is used as the second theme of the second movement, and the close of this theme is used to form a new melody with a violin obbligato above it. The trio of the scherzo is built from the theme of this violin obbligato, and the last movement of the symphony employs, in a new and striking form, the principal subject of the first movement.

Its plan of development.

This manner of writing a symphony leads directly to the symphonic poem, the invention of Franz Liszt. This form is based on the idea, which seems to have floated in Schumann's mind, that there is no break between successive emotional states. The form of a symphonic poem, therefore, is always dictated by the composer's emotional schedule. Usually this kind of composition aims to illustrate some story or poem, but the music-lover will find that the fundamental principles of musical form have to be followed. Slow movements alternate with quick ones; dynamic climaxes are opposed to points of repose, melodic subjects are proposed and discussed, and the symphonic poem has an appreciable musical shape.

The Symphonic poem.

Closely akin to this form is the programme overture, such as Tschaikowsky's "Hamlet" or Goldmark's "Prometheus." But in these also the attentive listener will find that the principles of form are not violated, though the outline of the works is not at all like that of the sonata. The difficulty in the way of immediate appreciation of the purely musical value of such compositions is the necessity of getting at the composer's emotional schedule. One has to have some key to the content of such works, and often in searching for it he loses his grip on the absolute music of the composition. Judicious programme notes are serviceable in such cases, for they convey the needed information as to the intention of the music. In the case of a composition without a story behind it, programme notes are of little value to the skilled listener.

A word should be added here as to Liszt's piano concertos, which have set the fashion for many succeeding works. In these the uninterrupted flow of movements and partial community of theme are employed with striking effect. The music itself is not of a lofty kind, but the form is very effective for concerto pur-

Romantic Forms

poses. It has a brilliancy and glitter which, while superficial, are very influential. But here again one finds that while the outward shape is novel, the underlying principles of form are those which are found in the classical works.

From what has been said the reader will have no difficulty in gathering that the mental and emotional characteristics of the romantic school embrace two fundamental conditions: First, subordination of form to content, and second, restlessness and intensity of emotional moods. The romantic school is the school of our time, and even the writer who adhered most closely to the classic forms, Johannes Brahms, aimed at an intensity of emotion similar to that found in Beethoven's later works. All that we can ask of the romantic composer is that his form shall be the best that can be devised for his purpose, and that it does not violate the primary canons of musical construction.

Traits of romantic music.

V

Fundamental Principles

HAVING seen the elements of form and their combination in the complex organism of the sonata, the most highly organized of all musical forms, it becomes possible now to view the general principles of musical form in the abstract. These should readily suggest themselves to the reader, who has now had a tolerably wide survey of the materials of musical design. In a simple song form the student will find that perfect balance in the arrangement of phrases, and natural, unforced progress of harmonies are imperative necessities. But it is to the more highly organized forms, as including the simpler ones, that I especially invite attention. The fundamental requisites of musical form, as gathered from the works of

Balance and design.

Fundamental Principles

the masters of sonata construction, are these:

1.—Proposition of themes suitable for development.
2.—Contrast (a) of themes, (b) of keys, (c) of movements.
3.—Development (a) of themes, (b) of harmony.
4.—Systematic distribution of repetitions with recurrence to first subject-matter.
5.—Climaxes, dynamic, rhythmic, and of time.
6.—Points of repose.
7.—Variety of tone-coloring.
8.—Correlation of parts and subordination of details = proportion.
9.—Perspicuity of design.

These principles, the reader will perceive, are not inseparable from the sonata form, but belong to all music which is of complex design. They underlie and condition not only the symphonies of Beethoven or Tschaikowsky, but those of Haydn. They govern the construction of both classic and romantic overtures and scherzos, and they are exemplified in the ballet music of Gluck, as

Chap. V.

Essentials of form.

Common to all music.

CHAP. V.

Small versus large forms.

well as in the ballades of Chopin or the novelettes of Schumann. In a fine sonata all of them are illustrated in the highest light, yet all of them are obeyed very often in much smaller compositions, and one must not be deluded into supposing that a sonata is better than other works simply because it is a sonata.

VOCAL FORMS

VI

Church Counterpoint

VOCAL forms can be discussed with comparative brevity, now that the general principles and development of form in music have been reviewed.

The growth of vocal forms in artistic music began with the mediæval church counterpoint, which, as we have already seen, was the work of monks, bent upon producing an effective liturgy. The early polyphonic compositions were all intended for voices, and their most elaborate development was in the Roman Catholic mass. The purely instrumental development of polyphony was begun by the early organists of the Venetian and Roman schools, and was perfected by Bach in his great fugues. At the outset, however, the vocal and the

Mediæval church music.

Essentials of vocal counterpoint.

instrumental treatments of polyphony were practically the same. The essentials of vocal church counterpoint are those of all polyphonic writing, and these have already been explained.

Beauty of church polyphony.

The finest examples of ecclesiastical polyphony are the works of the great Netherlands masters, who flourished from 1450 to 1600, and of Palestrina, the Italian composer, who was contemporary with the last lights of that school. Opportunities for hearing these works, the purest and loftiest church music ever composed, are not as numerous as music-lovers could wish. Those who desire to cultivate a fine taste in music should never miss hearing performances of the famous ecclesiastical compositions. From an educational point of view they are as important as Bach's fugues or Beethoven's symphonies. In mere sensuous beauty they far excel the former, and it is not possible to conceive of a musical ear that will not be ravished by the exquisite harmonies of these lovely works.

VII

Simple Song Forms

THE monophonic form of vocal music is found in the song and its varieties. Simple song forms, of which some description has already been given, date back to the very birth of music. The troubadours were cultivating them at the time when the scientific musicians were devoting their whole energy to the solution of riddle canons and the construction of polyphonic puzzles. The old folk-songs are admirable examples of this form in its simplest aspect. It will be seen upon examination of songs that the musical form is dictated by the poetic. The general principles of song form have already been explained, and the reader will, therefore, understand that a stanza of four lines calls for a song form of one period. A stanza of eight lines calls for

Age of the song.

Song form and poetry.

one of two periods, and the relation between the two periods is established by preserving the general character of the melody, the rhythmic movement, and the harmonic treatment. In a song form of three periods the composer may in the second period depart considerably from the original melodic style of the first period, but he must return to it in the third.

The cyclical song.

The three-period song form is cyclical, like the sonata, and its general contour is a diminished outline of the sonata form, the second period corresponding to the working out, and the third to the recapitulation. These forms belong to the songs in which each stanza is set to the same melody, as in folk-songs or ballads. In many modern songs, however, the composers have found it impossible to give adequate expression to the feelings conveyed by the text without making a melody for each stanza. The music-lover will find this the case with many of the songs of Schubert, Schumann, Franz, and other romantic writers. In

Meaning in accompaniment.

songs of this kind there is, indeed, always some repetition of the original melodic idea, but the unity of the com-

Simple Song Forms

position is to be found chiefly in its character. Often, as in Schubert's "Erl König," the formal element of repetition is preserved mostly in the accompaniment, yet there is an individuality in the style of the vocal melody from beginning to end.

It is difficult to speak of the formal qualities of a song separately from its other æsthetic properties, because the form is so important a part of the expressive power. The form and style are almost inseparable, and both are dictated by the subject-matter. The simpler the emotion to be portrayed, the simpler as a rule are the form and the style. Hence we find that songs range from those of a purely lyric nature, in which emotion is the product of pure contemplation, as in songs of night's beauty, the loveliness of spring, or the charms of a maiden, to those in which the dramatic element is almost as much in evidence as it is in opera, and in which emotion is the product of personal passion, as in Schubert's "Erl König" or "Doppelgänger," Schumann's "Ich grolle nicht," or Franz's "Im Herbst." The requirements of a

Value of form and style.

Dramatic songs.

Vocal Forms

CHAP. VII.

Essentials of a good song.

Variety of song forms.

genuinely good song are not numerous, but they are difficult to fulfil. A good song should reproduce perfectly the form of the poem, should be absolutely faithful to its spirit, should exhibit a lofty simplicity of style, should have a moderate compass, and should be supplied with an accompaniment thoroughly in sympathy with the emotional character of the work. The accompaniments of Schubert and Schumann are the perfect models. They always have lyric beauty and dramatic force, yet they never interfere with the voice-part, but, on the contrary, afford it complete support.

This brief discussion of the song runs beyond the consideration of its form alone, but it seems better to discuss the whole topic here and dismiss it. An exhaustive study of song forms and styles is foreign to the purpose of this volume, which aims at the exposition of general principles; and, furthermore, it would supply material for a volume in itself. Let us, therefore, proceed to a view of those vocal forms which are employed in dramatic music, and which have caused so much controversy.

VIII

Operatic Forms

APPRECIATION of opera depends not simply upon a knowledge of form, but upon an acquaintance with the nature and purpose of operatic music. This acquaintance may be obtained from two sources—musical history and an examination into the internal evidence of operatic music itself. Few persons have time to make such an examination, but the historical facts are easily ascertainable. Dramatic recitative, of which alone the opera at first consisted, was the invention of some Florentine enthusiasts who were endeavoring to resuscitate the Greek drama. Their intention in constructing recitative was to create a kind of musical declamation in which the melodic sequences should follow as closely as possible the inflections of the voice in speech.

Origin of opera.

Vocal Forms

Monotony of recitative.

Advent of the aria.

In a very short time it was found that this was a grave restriction on the freedom of composition, and that its results were wearisome. Almost at the same time the capacity of music for emotional expression forced its claims upon composers, and there was developed a free arioso style, a cross between pure recitative and melody, in which the imitation of speech was not sought so much as pure musical expression of emotion. The cyclical form of instrumental music now caught the fancy of composers for the stage and they transferred it to the opera, producing the aria, a tripartite song form, which became the central sun of the operatic system. The vital fault in the aria, as first written, was that the required repetition in the third part of the melody heard in the first, destroyed all possibility of a natural emotional continuity. No matter how agitated the soprano was in the second part of her aria, she had to feel in the third just the same as she did in the first.

The result was that the composers abandoned all thought of voicing emotion logically in an aria, and contented themselves with making all arias vocal display-pieces for the singers. The recitative was then used to carry on that part of the dialogue necessary to the development of the story of the opera. The custom of writing vocal display-pieces for the singers led to such a domination of the singer in opera, that operatic music became mere ear-tickling show-work, and composers became simply purveyors to the princes and princesses of the stage. A reaction at length set in, and, led by Gluck, composers reasserted the divine rights of genius. The recitative was improved and the arias simplified and restricted to their proper function of embodying states of emotion. Contemporary with Gluck was Mozart, whose operas exhibit the highest perfection of the old form. The arias are dramatic poems, and the recitative is the most finished musical setting of colloquial conversation that the stage has ever known.

Italian composers, however, again resorted to the easy process of tickling the ear without regard for the fitting of the melody to the text, and in the works of

Bellini, Donizetti, and Rossini we find much of this kind of writing. But recitative was constantly tending away from the Mozartian style toward the arioso. In the operas of the later Italian composers there is very little pure recitative, arioso and aria forms being chiefly employed. This led toward a movement to abolish all set forms from opera, which was carried to its achievement by Richard Wagner. In his later works there are no set arias, duets, or ensembles, but the musical form follows that of the text, which is written freely, as it would be in a spoken drama. The result is that the music embodies in a faithful manner the emotions of the text. The reader must now see that the purpose of artistic opera-music is to illustrate and vitalize the text. Unless it does this—or attempts to do it—operatic music is not an art form but an absurdity. It is accepted by the world simply as a part of the symbolism of art, for no one would accept as a fact the singing of personages in a play. But if the opera is not a play in which an attempt is made to express dramatic emotions in music, it is not an art-work at all. Hence, the first and fundamental basis of judgment of an opera is the fidelity of its music to the text. The second question to be answered is: How eloquently does the music voice the emotions contained in the text? And third: Is the music beautiful in itself?

The key to the music of an opera is the libretto. Obviously, if the libretto is weak or incongruous, the music is likely to be poor. The appropriateness of the music is the first requirement. If it is inappropriate, it does not make any difference how melodious or symmetrical it is, it is not good. It is by this test that so much of the old Italian opera-music fails, pretty as it is. The reason why so few people detect the hollowness of this music is that they do not hold it to the text. They read the libretto to learn the story of the opera, and that is all. But a critical view of an opera holds the composer to the text of every speech in it. Rossini's "Semiramide" affords the finest example of offence in this matter, and the reader who desires to know what an artistic opera should not be, will

Fidelity to the text.

Music as an expression.

do well to study the charming music of the score in the light of the text. The enormous vitality and powerful influence of Verdi's "Aida," on the other hand, is due to the honesty, more than to the beauty, of its music. Wagner's music dramas are the finest exponents of the true method of writing opera.

The reader will, perhaps, not be satisfied with this brief hint as to the nature and purpose of opera without the addition of some general remarks on the forms employed. Of recitative pure and simple there are two kinds, recitative *secco*, and recitative *stromentato*. Recitative *secco* is that in which there is absolutely no form except that of the text, the music being almost without rhythm or definite melody. The accompaniment consists wholly of detached chords, which are struck only when the harmony changes. In old times the double-bass and the harpsichord struck the chords, and it is customary now, in performances of Mozart's "Don Giovanni," in well-regulated opera-houses to play the chords of the recitative on a piano. Recitative *stromentato* is that which is accompanied throughout by the orchestra. In its most common form the instruments between the passages of recitative play illustrative melodic passages which bring out more clearly the feeling of the text. *Arioso* is a form of recitative in which there are passages of melody, without the formation of a complete air.

The *aria* has already been explained. The old form, in which the first part was always repeated, was called the *aria da capo*. Most modern *arias* are not *da capo*, but have a free repetition of the original subject-matter, as in the first tenor solo in "Aida"—"Celeste Aida." In modern operas *arias* are still written, because they are an essential part of opera, but they are in very free form, the form, indeed, being made for the occasion, as in Lohengrin's narrative, Siegmund's love-song, or Isolde's "liebestod." Of course these things are not *arias* in the old sense, but they stand in the same relation to music drama as the formal *aria* did to the old-fashioned opera. In the old operas the different kinds of *arias* had distinctive titles, as *aria di bravura,* an *aria* for the display of vocal agility (*vide* Lucia's mad scene); *aria parlante,* one in which there were passages resembling speech; *aria buffa,* a comic *aria,* as Leporello's "Madamina." The terms trio, quartet, and ensemble explain themselves. It is not the purpose of this volume to enter into a detailed description of forms, but to lay down general principles by which judgment may be guided and taste formed. The reader can find definitions of the various forms in any musical dictionary.

Let me call the reader's attention to one important point. Opera is the most popular form of musical entertainment, because in it the comprehension of music is made easy by means of pictures and text. But it is obviously not the highest form of music. In it music is only a component part of a whole, and it is governed absolutely by the text. The only artistic opera is that which Wagner described and aimed to write, that in which music, poetry, painting, and action are united in organic unity. Music is in this organic union precluded from the possibility of independent development.

Hence, I hold that the highest form of music is that in which music stands alone, and exercises her sway upon us wholly by means of her own unaided powers. Music unaccompanied by text is called absolute music, and this is surely the highest form of the art. It is for that reason that I have devoted my attention in this book chiefly to absolute music. It is for the same reason that I invite the reader who desires to arrive at an understanding and appreciation of musical art to study most zealously the great instrumental works.

CHAP. VIII.

Absolute music higher.

THE CONTENT OF MUSIC

IX

The Sensuous

Form not everything.

IT must be evident to the most careless listener to music that there is something more in the art than high organism of construction. Form is not all that inheres in music. If it were, the symphonies of Gyrowetz would live beside those of Beethoven, and the études of J. B. Cramer would be heard as often as those of Chopin. What qualities can the listener detect in music as evidence of its excellence? What phenomena of the art present themselves to us as a basis for critical judgment? I said at the outset that no rule could be laid down for recognizing the excellence of a musical idea. Neither can absolute rules be laid down for pronouncing judgments on complete compositions. Only the mind which has lived much with music, thought intensely about it, and absorbed its inner spirit can say with certainty in the presence of a work wholly novel in form and style, "This is good," or "This is bad." More than ninety-nine out of every hundred critics err in judgment of a thing wholly new in music, because the majority of them base their judgments almost altogether on form and style. Nevertheless, it is my belief that there is a substantial basis for musical criticism. I believe that criticism is reducible to method, and that every man is capable of perceiving and grasping the standards by which true musical art is to be measured. It may not be possible to lay down absolute rules for pronouncing judgments on musical compositions, but it is possible to get at certain fundamental qualities, and from them to deduce certain basic principles of art in music.

We have already reviewed Form, the constructive principle of artistic design, the method of development of musical thought, the logic of sound. But Form implies Content, otherwise we have an

CHAP. IX.

Criticism of form and style.

Fundamental qualities of music.

empty and soulless edifice, a cathedral of Gothic grandeur which does not express man's spiritual aspiration. Form and Content together make the Æsthetic of Musical Art. In their action and reaction upon one another, in their individual excellence and their combined significance, they produce the ultimate Truth and Beauty which are at once the subjects and the objects of all Art. In order that we may properly understand their relations, let us examine the fundamental forces of music, one of which includes, or rather produces, Form, and all of which are a part of the Content.

Three fundamental forces or qualities are inherent in music and claim consideration in respect of their effect upon the hearer. It is by the presence and amount of influence of these qualities that the artistic value of a composition must be estimated. If it can be shown that every one of these qualities is capable of employment in the composition of artistic music, it follows that the sum-total of the value of the composition cannot be estimated if any one of these factors is ignored. These three qualities are the

Sensuous, the Intellectual, and the Emotional.

The Sensuous embraces that part of music which appeals solely to the physical sense of hearing. It is that which in common parlance "tickles the ear." It affects hearing as the flavor of food affects taste, and the enjoyment of it is analogous to the enjoyment of edibles, such as cake or candy, without consideration of the nutritive properties. It is, of course, not quite possible to make a line of strict demarcation for the Sensuous in music because it so frequently works in close organization with the other qualities for a common end. Indeed, all three fundamentals are constantly present in the highest class of modern music, and one who measures the æsthetic value of a composition by the relative prominence given to each will not go far astray. For instance, if it be said that the strongest claim to attention in a given composition is its merely sensuous charm, then that composition is at once placed in the lowest class.

Music without any form whatever, without any evidence of constructive

CHAP. IX.

The sensuous element.

Purely sensuous music.

Sensuousness of the orchestra.

design, without emotional content, and without the æsthetic manifestations of symmetry, grace, or strength, might, nevertheless, be full of sensuous charm, by reason of its various bits of pretty melody, its rich harmony, or its highly colored instrumentation. Indeed, it is in orchestral music that one is most likely to be deceived by the purely sensuous quality of music, for the palette of the modern symphonist is full of gorgeous colors, and a very poor piece of composition may be made to sound imposing by the cunning employment of divided violins with harmonies of horns and harp, by ingeniously dispersed chords for the wood-wind, or by the thunderous shock of a solid tutti. In solo work, however, the sensuous element plays an equally deceptive part. A contralto who committed every offence against the rules of vocal art was successful on the operatic stage for years by reason of the engaging quality of her voice. A pianist who read the works of Chopin in a manner most erratic carried away the public by the beauty of his tone-coloring.

The Sensuous is that part of music

The Sensuous

which makes its appeal triumphantly to the indolent or unintelligent listener. He does not wish to understand music. He wishes only to hear it. He abhors its intellectual attributes, and of course its true emotion never reaches him. He refuses to trouble his mind sufficiently to detect evidences of design in the work. He reduces music to the level of confectionery. The sweetness and the flavor of it are all that he loves. He takes it as the school-girl takes her novel. If the ending be happy, what cares she for the purity of the diction, the picturesqueness of the descriptions, the fidelity of the character-drawing, the profound insight into human life? So the thoughtless music-hearer, if the tunes be pretty, the rhythms incisive, and the voice-timbres rich, cares not a fig whether there is thematic development, organic life, or deep feeling in the work. Yet out of the Sensuous is great music made.

This Sensuous part of music embraces all that first appeals to the ear—rhythm, melody, harmony, tone-color. In and of themselves these factors are simply sen-

Pleasure of the thoughtless.

The Content of Music

Chap. IX.

Factors of the Sensuous.

suous. Unorganized, without design, without form, but employed simply to fascinate the sense of hearing, to make "a dance of sound," these factors descend to their lowest use, and music so composed can hardly be said to be music at all. Yet melody, rhythm, and harmony are the elements of musical form. They are the material out of which its highest organizations are developed. They are sensuous when they are used as a painter might use the Hogarthian line of beauty and the entire Winsor & Newton catalogue of colors to fashion a kaleidoscopic canvas which should give to the eye the same sort of delight that a gas-light gives to the vision of a babe. The painter would advance a step when he combined his lines and colors into some recognizable form—say, a tree or a rose. But he would not then produce a composition. That would

Composition and painting.

come only in a work which combined several recognizable forms, such as trees, roses, grass, clouds, and perhaps a human figure or two, in a work with evident design.

And so in music melody, rhythm,

and harmony cease to be mere sensuous things when they work together in a piece of constructive composition. Even tone-color, the most absolutely sensuous factor of all, ceases to be simply that when it is employed with an intellectual or an emotional purpose. But tone-color, being the most sensuous, and therefore the most easily dazzling, is the factor which is most abused in recent music. The noble artistic reticence of Beethoven, whose tonal schemes are full of the solid yet subdued glory of Corot's landscapes, is seldom found in new orchestral works, many of which seek to cover up barren melodic subjects, feeble development, and insincere emotion with Turneresque outpours of gorgeous color. Chamber music seeks to rival orchestral in the complexity of its polyphony, and the variety of its tone tints, while the piano aims at tonal dictatorship.

The laws which govern the employment of the Sensuous in music belong partly to the Intellectual, and partly to the Emotional. The Sensuous is their servant, and must obey their commands. It is a means, not an end. All that is

The Content of Music

Chap. IX.

Color and Outline.

embraced in it belongs fairly to the material of the art, and this must be subservient to thought and feeling. Especially is this true of the most sensuous part of the Sensuous, the color scheme. For while we admit the undoubted existence of a rule that there should be sensuous variety, we must also admit that this rule is subservient to the laws of melodic and harmonic development, and that the color must never be out of keeping with the outline. The purple cow or the green carnation is always an inartistic monstrosity.

X

The Intellectual

A MOST important part of the Intellectual quality of music has already been discussed under the head of Form, for it is not difficult to perceive that the Intellectual embraces that part of composition which discloses purpose, and produces logical construction. Ambros, in his excellent work, "The Boundaries of Poetry and Music," designates the music of the romantic school as the "music of the intellect," and that of the early classicists as the "music of the soul." By this he means to convey the idea that the classicists gave their souls free play, and that those souls revelled in pure musical beauty, while the romanticists, in endeavoring to make music voice emotions definitely, displayed a purely intellectual method. But a little reflec-

"Music of the intellect."

CHAP. X.

Intellect and method.

The Intellectual and design.

tion should make it obvious that there are fundamental intellectual qualities in all music. They are to be found in some measure in the emotionless works of Ockeghem, as well as in the sunny, genial symphonies of Haydn. They are present in all the classic compositions, side by side with the emotional qualities. Yet Ambros is in a measure right, for the more definitely a composer aims at making his music an expression of emotion, the more firmly must he fashion it according to the dictates of intellect, for were he to attempt emotional expression without preserving the supremacy of the reason in his work, he would speedily fall into formlessness, and instead of enlightening would merely bewilder his hearers. In all art creative, or interpretative, the emotion must be under the dominance of the reason, or else there is no method, and art without method is inconceivable.

The Intellectual in music, then, embraces first all the principles of design, the laws of form and development. But rising from the specific laws of form to the generic principle which lies at the

The Intellectual

basis of the Intellectual in music we find that the ultimate aim of design in the tone art is organic unity, that unity in diversity which, as Mr. Hadow* pertinently reminds us, it was the chief aim of Greek philosophy to discover in Nature. The requirement of organic unity is that details of diverse character shall be absolutely vital parts of one organism. In a work of art this requirement demands that no accessory shall be foreign to the general design. In music it especially demands that the form shall be perfect, that the whole shall be equal to the sum of all its parts, that nothing can be subtracted without causing imperfection, and that nothing can be added to what is already complete. It calls for an absolutely reasonable development of each movement from its germinal melodic ideas. It demands that those germs shall be developed to the full measure of their fruitfulness, but that there shall be no overripeness. It orders that no extraneous matter shall obtrude itself upon the attention, and that if new

Chap. X.

Demands of musical design.

---
* "Studies in Modern Music," by W. H. Hadow, M.A., Second Series.

CHAP. X.

A correct emotional scheme.

Attributes of an organism.

thought is introduced it shall clearly grow out of the ideas first propounded. It furthermore demands that the emotional scheme of a movement shall not be incongruous, but shall follow accepted psychological laws. It goes still farther and commands that the several movements of a work shall be organically related to one another in melodic character, emotional mood, and in style. If you were to hear the scherzo of Beethoven's Seventh Symphony performed in the Fifth Symphony instead of that which belongs there, you would detect the inorganic conditions at once. As Ambros has wisely said, no one has ever found the "Eroica" symphony unheroic, or the "Pastoral" unpastoral, but there would be an immediate outcry if the titles were transposed.

Mr. Hadow, whose works I heartily commend to every sincere lover of music, quotes Herbert Spencer on the three main attributes of an organism. "First, it must be definite, clear in outline, complete in substance, and filling with unbroken continuity the fixed limits by which it is circumscribed. Secondly, it must be heterogeneous: composed, that is, of a plurality of parts, each of which has its own function, and no two of which are interchangeable. Thirdly, it must be coherent: holding this plurality in exact balance and equipoise, so that each part, incapable by itself of maintaining the whole body, is yet essential to the due health and efficiency of the others." As Mr. Hadow justly says, "It is to music that the law of organic proportion most intimately applies," and the construction of a musical organism is a purely intellectual accomplishment. The conception of musical ideas may be, and in great music generally is, the result of some emotional state, but the fashioning of a composition and all that belongs to that task are intellectual; and in music the intellectual element issues in Form, because Form is the *method* of expression.

So important have the higher attributes of musical form appeared to some critics, that they have declared form to be expression. The most notable advocate of this view is Dr. Eduard Hanslick, whose "Beautiful in Music" aims to prove that music is nothing more than

CHAP. X.

The Intellectual in history.

sounding forms, that it is incapable of emotional expression, and that its highest attributes are intellectual. The book is worth study, if for no other purpose than to learn how highly the Intellectual in music may be estimated by some who have loved the art all their lives. But it is difficult to understand how any close student of music and its history can fail to perceive that emotion has been present in the tone art almost from its birth. In the early history of music we find that the necessity of making the materials of the art kept the Intellectual in the foreground until composers had sufficiently mastered their material to enable them to seek for pure euphony of tones, and then the Sensuous joined the Intellectual. When these two elements had become sufficiently plastic in the hands of the masters, music disclosed a purpose, and that purpose was plainly the expression of feeling. In the days of the *a capella* church writers, the feeling was purely religious and contemplative. In the days of the strictly classic writers the emotions continued to be of the simpler kind, and it was regarded as sufficient for a movement to be in a general mood throughout. But with Beethoven, the Columbus who opened up a new world to the art, there entered a definite intellectual method of expressing emotions, and a sonata became an epic, with each movement a canto surcharged with a variety of emotions.

Yet there can be no question of the artistic unity of each work. The organism is always complete and vital, and it is so not simply because Beethoven perceived more clearly than Mozart and Haydn the emotional expressiveness of music, but equally because he perfected the intellectual processes of expression. To Beethoven we owe the completed sonata form, the highest organism of unaided music. He carried that form to its furthest influence, but he did not preclude the possibility of the development of other forms. What he did was to embody in the sonata the fundamental principles of all Form in music, and it is because Form is essentially intellectual method in this art that I lay so much stress upon the necessity of acquaintance with its laws.

XI

The Emotional

THE power of music to express emotion has been denied, but it is not the purpose of the present volume to reopen the discussion of that question. The controversy over the expressive power of music may be regarded as closed. The artistic world has agreed that music does convey emotion, or feeling of some kind, and that it arouses feeling in the hearer. The theory that the aroused feeling is of a nervous kind, caused wholly by the physical effects of melody and rhythm, has already been overthrown, and, indeed, it never had much weight with those who were capable of psychological self-examination.

There is no doubt, however, that most people have vague and unsettled ideas as to the expressive powers of music,

Music arouses emotion

and that in looking for something that does not exist, they fail to find that which does. This vagueness arises from three causes: First, ignorance of the true nature of musical expressiveness; second, ignorance of musical history, which leads them to look for effects not sought by composers of certain periods; and third, foolish and rhapsodical criticism, which pretends to see definite poetic imagery in music. A correct understanding of the true nature of musical expressiveness would at once expose the fallacy of such criticism. It is my intention to point out, as briefly as possible, what constitutes the emotional content of music. It will, perhaps, lead to a readier comprehension of this to indicate in a general way the materials of emotional expression in this art.

The reader will remember that under the head of Form it was stated that song was originally a free expression of fancy or feeling, and that the melodic intervals were based on the inflections of the voice in speech. It can be shown without great difficulty that this primary law of musical expression lies at the

Mistakes about musical emotion.

Primary law of expression.

CHAP. XI.

Music imitates speech.

base of the most imposing symphonies or symphonic poems. For instance, the minor keys are usually employed to express grief. Why? Because the inflections of the human voice in expression of sorrow usually ascend and descend through intervals closely resembling those of the minor scale. Still more poignant grief, that which has a note of tragic passion in it, is expressed by chromatic harmonies. Why? Because the human voice in speaking such grief actually moves through the chromatic scale. High, shrieking sounds are suitable to the expression of stormy feelings because we so express them with our voices, while dark and gloomy feelings call for low, suppressed tones. Again, in calm, contemplative speech the voice flows smoothly and equably. And such a mood would call for a steadily maintained rhythm and a moderate tempo. In an agitated mood the speech does not flow, but is spasmodic and irregular; hence music imitates speech with complex rhythm, with staccato chords, *rinforzandi*, and syncopations.

These few comparisons are sufficient

to show the thoughtful reader that the means of musical expression are not altogether arbitrary, but are founded on natural law. But because music has more complex machinery than the human voice, it can achieve more complex expression. Its compass is wider, its variety of tone-color is greater, its dynamic force is higher, its number of rhythms is larger, and it has harmony, which the voice has not. The intensity and power of the utterance of an orchestra, for instance, far exceeds that of any orator or singer. By the powerful projection through song of a singer's personality, we are often misled into supposing that the human voice is the most expressive of all instruments; but pure musical expressiveness exists in its highest degree in the orchestra, where the influence is not personal, but absolutely musical.

But music has no articulate speech. For that reason it is compelled to express emotions in the abstract. The composer can say to you, "I am sad," and in saying it he can influence you to be sad with him. But he cannot say to

Chap. XI.

Power of musical expression.

Limit of this expression.

you in music, "I am sad because my brother is dead." The materials of musical expression do not admit of such definite statement. Music can speak a sadness more intense than words can utter, but it is the privilege of the poet, not of the musician, to tell the cause of the sadness. Music, then, is an art which expresses moods, and it expresses them with definiteness, tremendous eloquence, and overwhelming influence. The mistake of those who are ignorant of the real nature of musical expressiveness is that they try to discern in the music the cause of the moods, and this we have seen is just what music cannot tell us. As Ambros has admirably said: "Music conveys moods of finished expression; it, as it were, forces them on the hearer. It conveys them in *finished* form, because it possesses no means for expressing the previous series of ideas which *speech* can clearly and definitely express. The charm of music, which one is so very much inclined to ascribe to sensuous euphony alone, lies, in a great measure, if not for the most part, in this contrasting

The Emotional

of finished states of mind, concerning whose previous series of ideas it gives us no account."

That the expressive power of music is none the less definite is easily demonstrable. No one would mistake the slow movement of Tschaikowsky's "Symphony Pathetique" for a hymn to joy, and equally no one would think Beethoven's melody for Schiller's "Hymn to Joy" in the last movement of the Ninth Symphony was a lament. The graceful, contemplative mood of Schubert's "Hark, hark, the lark," could never be mistaken for the tragic feeling of Beethoven's sonata, opus 106. The attitude of the hearer, I repeat, is what leads to error. When he asks, "What does this music express?" nine times out of ten he wishes to know what caused the composer's emotion. It is not always impossible to learn that, but it must be learned from a study of the composer's life, not from his music. As the author has said in another place: "Who has solved the riddles of Beethoven's last quartets and sonatas? Their interpretation must rest upon a sympathetic

Chap. XI.

Not an indefinite expression.

Errors of the hearer.

CHAP. XI.

Groundless expectations.

What one may expect.

study of the emotional life of the composer at the time they were conceived. Tell us what Beethoven suffered or dreamed while he wrote any one of these works, and you have offered us a key to his meaning."

The mistake of those who know nothing of musical history is that they seek in the older works for an intensity of emotional expressiveness not attempted by the composers, and either wholly misunderstand the works by fancying they find it, or are disappointed by what appears to be their weakness. It was because of the existence of this error that the author called attention to the mental and emotional characteristics of the three great periods of music. One must not seek for anything beyond contemplative or religious emotion in the works of the early contrapuntists. With Haydn the emotional schedule is broader, yet here the gentler feelings, mingled with unaffected gayety and genial humor, abound. Tragedy is not found in the Haydn symphonies or quartets, nor is it in those of Mozart, whose emotional schedule was still wider than that of Haydn. But with all the classic writers pure musical beauty was the chief end of the art, and the emotional scheme had to remain subservient to the laws of form. It was Beethoven who first definitely aimed at making emotional utterance the purpose of music, and from his time dates the development of the knowledge of the full resources of the tone art as the wordless poetry of the soul.

Beethoven's emotional utterance.

The misfortune of those who fall victims to bad commentary is that they are induced to read into music definite images which are contrary to the nature of the art, and are simply the product of the fancy of one person. Permit me to quote a passage of the sort of comment to which I refer. It is from a description of Beethoven's Seventh Symphony:

Evils of bad criticism.

> "The longed-for moment is drawing near, and in blissful anticipation of the approaching consummation of their wishes, the graceful spirit-shapes move about playfully, now ascending, now descending (Bar 21 and the following, before *allegro*), until at length they are loudly bidden to begin the round-dance. They hesitate, bashfully at first, as though

loath to divulge their secret (the last bars before the *allegro*). Suddenly a slight tremor passes through their ranks. It is the last trepidation of joy, preceding its fullest outward manifestation which now ensues. Louder and louder the summons to the general jubilation issues forth; higher and higher still the waves of enjoyment rise; closer and ever closer their spirits join each other in the dance and unite their voices in a song of rapture. The first delirium of ecstatic joy over, the magic measure of *individual* tone-spirits is displayed. And alike in the sweet accents of the flute, in the loud blast of the trumpet, and in the gentle tone of the horn, the secret of every one of them becomes manifest. Then (with the organ-point upon E) the spirits again unite in loving embrace, resuming their song of joy with dithyrambic fervor."

Of course the person who, having read that, tries to discover in the Seventh Symphony a story of spirits engaged in a dance will meet with certain disappointment, and if he does not blame himself for the failure he will blame the music. It is obvious that the censure should fall upon the commentator, who found his explanation not in the music but in his own imagination.

Certain conventions, however, have been established in musical expression, and these are at once intelligible. For

The Emotional

instance, a slow march in a minor key with the beats heavily marked and the tone-color dark is universally accepted now as a funeral march. "Thoughts of religious functions arise in us the moment we hear the trombones intone a solemn phrase in full harmony; an oboe melody in six-eighth time over a drone bass brings up a pastoral picture of a shepherd playing upon his pipe; trumpets and drums suggest war, and so on." * Motion is easily imitated by music, and there are conventional ways of imitating the rolling of waves, the galloping of horses, and the rippling of forest leaves. But the thoughtful music-lover will easily perceive that these purely imitative processes are materialistic, and that descriptive music only becomes spiritually influential when it embodies in the imitation of a natural object the emotions which it causes. A splendid example of this is Siegfried's forge song, in which the music, embodying the rhythm of the bellows, also expresses the splendid vigor and enthusiasm of the young

CHAP. XI.

Conventions of expression.

Descriptive music.

---

* "How to Listen to Music," by H. E. Krehbiel.

smith. Pure description in music without emotional content is the lowest form of musical expression. It is imitation, not utterance. It is objective, and all high music is subjective.

These considerations afford us a tolerably sure ground for our estimates of compositions belonging to the class known as "programme music." Under the head of Form it was stated that programme music was intended to illustrate some story or poem. After what has been said about the emotional expressiveness of music, the reader will perceive that the use of a suggestive title, or of a story, is simply a method of giving the hearer a definite cause for the emotions contained in a composition. Goldmark's "Sakuntala" overture, for instance, would be just as admirable a composition and just as strong in emotional expression if it were called simply "Concert Overture." But by his title the composer invites us to accept the Sanskrit poem as the cause of the particular series of emotions here conveyed to us in music.

Plainly, the excellence of any piece

The Emotional

of programme music logically depends upon the suitability of the story to broad emotional treatment, and upon the composer's ability to grasp the fundamental moods of the story and paint them in tones. He cannot tell the story; he can only voice its feelings. If some one of the natural objects for which musical conventions exist plays an important part in the story, he may use the descriptive convention with good effect. But he cannot become a novelist and give us scenery, action, and incident. He must adhere to his art and sing the contents of the heart. The opera composer can have the help of text, scenery, and action. They tell the story. It is the composer's business to project the emotions of the characters and make the auditors of his music feel them. An opera libretto is good when, like that of "Tristan und Isolde," it deals in broad, powerful scenes of pure, human emotion, because then the composer's task is one within the scope of his art.

So, operatic music is to be valued precisely according to the power and beauty with which it unfolds the emo-

CHAP. XI.

Communication of emotion.

tions indicated by the text. The same law applies to programme music. As I have said elsewhere, however, "the highest form of programme music is that in which the programme is simply an emotional schedule. I mean that the composer, having studied his own soul, and having found that certain events in his life or observation have given rise to a train of emotions, designs his composition to convey some knowledge of that train of emotions to his hearer, and to place him in responsive sympathy with it. He says to the hearer, 'Listen to my music and feel what I have felt.'"

XII

Æsthetics of Music

THE groundwork of the broad, essential principles of the æsthetics of music has now been explored, and we are ready, following the inductive method, to formulate some of the fundamental laws of musical beauty. It is generally conceded that an art-work should be beautiful, but there is considerable difference of opinion as to what constitutes beauty. It is the opinion of the present writer that on this topic the utterance of the great German philosopher, Immanuel Kant, is the most satisfactory. He holds that "the Beautiful is that which, through the harmony of its form with the faculty of human knowledge, awakens a disinterested, universal, and necessary satisfaction." By disinterestedness in relation to beau-

What is the beautiful?

ty, Kant means freedom from gratification of sensual appetite or preconceived conceptions. The Beautiful gives pleasure, not because it satisfies any physical appetite or corresponds to any extant idea, but because in and through itself it imprints its own Ideal upon the soul, which, by its faculty of knowledge, is capable of receiving it. By universal satisfaction Kant means that which is not peculiar to the individual, but is general. The satisfaction is necessary in the sense that it is inevitable. It must be borne in mind that Kant is speaking of general law, not of individual instances.

Kant furthermore distinguishes between *free* and *adherent* beauty. "Free beauty presupposes no conception of that which the object ought to be; merely adherent beauty implies both such a conception and also the perfection of the object as determined by comparison with the conception." Now it seems to me perfectly obvious that music, beyond all other arts, supplies us with both free and adherent beauty. The absolute musical concept, the melodic idea, does not, and in the very nature of its existence cannot, presuppose any conception of what it ought to be. No human being could have determined beforehand what kind of a theme Beethoven should invent as the principal subject of the Fifth Symphony, yet the moment it is heard, "through the harmony of its form with the faculty of human knowledge," that theme certainly does awaken "a disinterested, universal, and necessary satisfaction."

Free beauty in music, then, is that which belongs to its germinal conceptions. The adherent beauty is that which belongs to its expression and must be sought in the Sensuous and the Intellectual. The emotional content of music is not merely a part of its beauty; it is also a cause of it, for it is that which the art symbolizes. All art is symbolical, and the emotional content of music bears precisely the same relation to its beauty as the character which a portrait painter reveals in his portrait or the mood of Nature which a landscape-painter shows in a landscape does to the picture. A musical composition which

CHAP. XII.

Free and adherent beauty.

Their place in music.

Art and symbolism.

symbolized in a most convincing musical manner a series of incongruous emotions would fail to awaken Kant's satisfaction, not because the musical ideas in themselves were ugly, nor because the expression was incomplete, but because the matter symbolized was untrue. It would be like a tropical landscape with a frozen river in the foreground—not a work of art, but a curiosity.

The first law of musical æsthetics, then, is that a composition must contain free beauty. The melodic ideas must in and of themselves be beautiful. As I said at the beginning of this work, no rule can be laid down for recognizing the excellence of a musical idea. Such recognition belongs to the intuitions of the mind. I am well aware that in saying this I contradict a general belief that people have to be educated up to a recognition of excellence in musical ideas. That, however, is only true of people who have been educated down to

Beauty and education.

something else. People who have been brought up on dance music, variety-stage songs, and music-hall ditties have to be educated up to Beethoven and

Wagner. So do people who have never been in the presence of any art at all, musical or pictorial. But even these people very speedily learn to perceive the superiority of Beethoven's melodic ideas to those of David Braham.

But free beauty, which appeals to an indefinable consciousness of vitality, is not enough. A work of art must appeal to the judgment, which is an intellectual power. The very word art indicates something in which skill, thought, effort, and taste are exercised, and the perception of the results of such exercise is the labor of reason. Hence, a musical composition must have adherent beauty, and that beauty is surely to be found chiefly in the qualities which have been described as intellectual. But in musical art the adherent beauty of the intellectual development in a composition has a singular quality of its own. It does not satisfy us so much by its agreement with a preconceived conception of what it ought to be as by an immediate conviction that it could not have been other than what it is. This is one of the finest traits of a great composition. It must

Art and judgment.

Value of the Inevitable.

possess the element of Inevitableness. In listening to such a work as Beethoven's Fifth Symphony, we feel that every phrase is inevitable. To have written it otherwise would have weakened the structure. This Inevitableness is produced by perfection of form, by absolute logic of development, and is, therefore, an intellectual quality.

Closely related to it is the principle of Fitness, on which Mr. Hadow lays much stress. But this Fitness is almost wholly concerned with style, and may be dismissed briefly. This principle demands that the manner shall be suitable to the matter. It not only forbids the employment of a secular style in sacred music, but it prohibits the juxtaposition of incongruous styles in any work. For instance, imagine the working-out part of a Beethoven sonata written in a Chopinesque manner. Or fancy a sonata built of music like that of Rossini's "Semiramide." The thing would be a burlesque on music. It may be said, however, that the principle of Fitness applied to vocal music demands that the musical ideas shall be appropriate to the text.

This means, of course, that the music shall be as complete and life-like an embodiment as possible of the emotions set forth by the poet. It is the principle which lies at the basis of opera, and adherence to it is the only excuse which operatic writing has for its existence. Opera music which does not voice the emotions of the text is empty jingle. It may be melodious and symmetrical in form, but it is insincere, it is not inevitable, it is not fit, and hence it is not artistic. Its appeal is chiefly to the ear, and its beauty is mainly sensuous.

Fitness in opera music.

It is hardly necessary to add anything to what has already been said about the emotional part of a composition. The reader will speedily perceive that the chief law is that the emotional schedule should not embrace anything incapable of being expressed in music. The whole range of elementary emotions is open to the composer, if he will only content himself with treating them in the abstract. He must not try to tell the cause of the emotion; he needs text when he aims at that. And he must not try to represent purely intellectual proc-

Æsthetics of the emotional.

esses. I need hardly add that great emotions should be found in a great composition.

The conception of Beauty, as Kant notes, belongs to man alone. The beasts do not share it with him. Now, music is wholly the creation of the human intellect. It has no model in Nature as painting and sculpture have. The very materials of music are the products of man's thought. Because Beauty is conceived only by man, and music is the pure product of his intellect, it seems to me that this art comes nearer to an expression of beauty in the abstract than any other. It is the highest product of the imagination, and hence closer to free beauty than any other art. It proceeds out of the elements of our tripartite nature, sensation, reason, and emotion, in their most uncircumscribed and unconditioned state, and consequently it appeals to them with irresistible force.

As symmetry, proportion, balance, and logical development are essential to the perfection of an art-work, and as these are the results of design, no composition can be truly great, no matter how notable the free beauty of its germinal ideas or how eloquent its expression of emotion unless it is built according to the fundamental laws of Form. The musical conceptions and the play of emotions must be alike governed by the reason. Of the genuine composer it must always be said as Martin Luther said of the great pupil of Ockeghem: "Other composers have to do as the notes let them, but Josquin is master of the notes." And so we come at last to the true balance of parts in a musical art-work, a balance pre-existent in the tripartite nature of man. A great man is one who has a great body and a great soul absolutely ruled by principle, which is a product of reason. A great composition is one in which there are sensuous beauty and emotional eloquence, governed by the laws of Form.

Summary of musical beauty.

Part II

The Performance of Music

INSTRUMENTAL PERFORMANCE.

XIII

The Orchestra

WHILE the lover of music may often be in doubt as to the merit of a composition, he need never be so in regard to that of a performance. Here we stand on safe and sure ground, for the qualities that make excellence in performance are all well known, and it is necessary only that the ear shall be able to detect them. There may, of course, be some difference of opinion about the reading of a sonata or the interpretation of a symphony; but even these differences should be rare. Differences of judgment about the technical qualities of a musical performance should never exist. Whether a person plays the piano or sings well or ill is not a ques-

Performance a sure ground.

CHAP. XIII.

Questions of fact.

tion of opinion, but of fact. The critic who is acquainted with the technics of the art can pronounce judgment upon a performance with absolute certainty, and there is no reason in the world why every lover of music should not do the same thing. There should not be any room for such talk as this: "I think Mrs. Blank sang very well, didn't you?" "Well, I didn't like it much."

And there should be no room for the indiscriminate applause of bad performances which so often grieve the hearts of judicious listeners. Bad orchestral playing, bad piano playing, bad singing are applauded every day in the course of the musical season by people who think they have a right to an opinion. I repeat that it is not a matter of opinion but a matter of fact; and a person might just as well express the belief that a short fat man was finely proportioned as to say that an ill-balanced orchestra was a good one, and he might as well say that in his opinion a fire-engine whistle was music as to say that a throaty voice-production was good singing.

In the second part of this little volume, therefore, I propose to set forth, as briefly as possible, the essentials of good performance for the information of those who, not knowing them, have not the grounds for judgment. Instrumental performance will be considered first, and it is natural to study first of all the greatest of all instruments—the orchestra.

The modern orchestra is the result of a long development, which it would not be profitable to trace in this book. It is a body of instruments, selected with a view to their ability to perform the most complex music. It will be readily understood that such an instrumental body must possess a wide range of timbres, a great compass, extensive gradations of force, the greatest flexibility, and a solid sonority which can be maintained from the finest pianissimo to the heaviest forte. Of course the preservation of some of these qualities, such as flexibility and solidity, depend largely upon the skill of the composer, but they are all inherent in the orchestra. They are gained by the use of three classes of instruments, grouped under the general

CHAP. XIII.

Its three groups.

The various instruments.

heads of wood, brass, and strings, which have special tone-colors and individuality when heard in their distinct groups, but which combine admirably in the ensemble.

It is the custom to name the three groups in the order given because, for the sake of convenience, composers place the flute parts at the top of the page of the score when the wide margin gives room for their high notes. The other wood-wind instruments follow the flutes, so as to keep the wood-choir together. The brass is placed under the wood because its members are so often combined with some of the wood instruments in sounding chords. This brings the strings to the bottom of the page, the instruments of percussion (drums, cymbals, etc.) being inserted between them and the brass.

The instruments of the conventional symphonic orchestra of the classic period, then, are flutes, oboes, clarinets, bassoons in the wood department, horns, trumpets, and trombones in the brass, and violins, violas, violoncellos, and double-basses for strings. Modern composers have added for special reasons the English horn, which is the alto of the oboe, the bass-clarinet, the contra-bassoon (which sounds an octave lower than the ordinary bassoon), the bass-tuba, a powerful double-bass brass instrument, and the harp. The piccolo, a small, shrill flute sounding an octave higher than the ordinary flute, was introduced into the symphony orchestra by Beethoven, though it had frequently been used before in opera scores.

It is not possible to convey in print any idea of the timbres of the various instruments. These are only to be learned by hearing them, and the simplest plan is to get a friend who knows the different instruments by sound to identify them for you. Something may be said, however, about the functions of the three choirs. The wood-wind used to be employed with very little skill until Mozart introduced the art of instrumental coloring. This he did by employing different wood-wind instruments in solo passages and in combinations. Any person will readily understand that a flute has a different tone from an oboe or a clarinet; but few stop to think how

Functions of the three choirs.

much difference in color can be obtained by sounding a flute with an oboe instead of with a clarinet. It is by making different combinations of instruments that different tone-colors are produced in an orchestra, and for this purpose the wood-choir is especially well adapted.

Now this choir, as a whole, is capable of playing by itself in full harmony, as in the music of Elsa's entrance to the cathedral, or the exit of Elizabeth in the third act of "Tannhäuser." It is capable, also, of subdivision into small groups, each of which can produce harmony and melody. For instance, two flutes and two oboes, or two flutes and two clarinets, or two oboes and two bassoons, or two clarinets and two bassoons may be used, and each of these combinations can play a melody built on full chords of four tones. Again, the whole of the wood can be employed in combination with all the strings or all the brass, or with parts of either. In tutti passages (those written for the entire orchestra) all the wood-wind instruments are used, though their individuality of tone is lost in the general mass of sound.

Flutes and oboes are purely soprano instruments, while bassoons cover the bass and baritone registers and part of the tenor. Clarinets are both soprano and contralto, their low tones being of singular depth and richness, but of sombre tint. The instruments are generally employed in pairs, but in modern works a third flute, a third clarinet, and a third bassoon are often found, and sometimes a fourth. The older composers always wrote their wood-wind parts in one manner, putting the flutes and oboes uppermost, the former usually doubling the latter in the octave, and both sounding what may be described as the soprano and alto parts of the chord. The clarinets filled in the middle notes, and the bassoons played the bass. This produced a close harmony, upon which no improvement can be made in tutti passages. But late writers use a dispersed harmony, making the compass of their chords much greater, and the intervals between the neighboring tones wider. This is a method which produces much

CHAP. XIII.

Its compass and variety.

Close and dispersed writing.

CHAP. XIII.

The brass choir.

French horn passages.

beauty and variety of color, and in Wagner's music it causes those rich organ-like effects which are so lovely.

The list of brass instruments used in the contemporaneous orchestra comprises four horns, two trumpets, and three trombones. Others are frequently added, the most familiar being the bass-tuba in E-flat. The French horn, as it is usually called, is the old mediæval hunting-horn adapted for orchestral use. It is a most valuable instrument by reason of the refined nobility and gentle sadness of its tone, when used in solos. It is beyond question the most expressive of the brass instruments, and its variety of color is so wide that it can give a good imitation of a thundering trombone, or unite excellently in soft chords with strings, or clarinets and bassoons. The older composers used two horns, but now it is customary to employ four of them. When not used for solo purposes, the horns generally sustain long chords in support of other instruments. Frequently the horn quartet is heard alone. Familiar horn passages, by which anyone may identify the tone of the instrument, are the trio in the scherzo of the "Eroica," and the hunting calls previous to the entrance of the Landgrave in Act I. of "Tannhäuser."

The trumpets, usually replaced by cornets, are the sopranos of the brass choir. Their brilliant, militant tone is familiar. They are used in chords and in enforcing tutti passages. They are seldom given the melody except when the brass plays alone or leads the orchestra. The three trombones, alto, tenor, and bass, are used chiefly to sustain harmonies, but they are capable of fine effect in broad melodic passages, as in the pilgrims' chorus in the "Tannhäuser" overture. The tuba is the double bass of the brass band, and plays the lowest notes of the harmonies. It is not necessary to say much about the character of the brass. Everyone is familiar with it. But it is a great mistake to suppose that brass is always noisy simply because it is used to make a volume of tone in tutti passages. Its effect when played softly is incomparably fine, as may be noted in the prayer in "Lohengrin."

The instruments of percussion speak

Trumpets and trombones.

CHAP. XIII.

Use of kettle drums.

The string quintet.

for themselves. They are all used to accentuate rhythms, except the kettle-drums (called tympani), which can be tuned to certain tones. The low drum has a compass from F below the bass-clef to the middle C, and the high drum from B-flat up to F on the fourth line. A great many striking effects are obtained by skilful use of the tympani, as, for examples, the use of one drum to play the bass to the melody of flutes and violins in the andante of Beethoven's First Symphony, and the same master's employment of two drums tuned an octave apart in the scherzo of the Ninth.

The string-choir is usually spoken of as the quartet, though it is really a quintet. Its most important instrument is the violin, the prima donna of the orchestra. Its clear, penetrating tones make it the richest voice of the orchestra, and a mass of violins playing in the upper or middle register make the most brilliant color in the instrumental palette. The compass of violins, which extends from the C below the treble-clef to C in the sixth space above the staff, is increased by the use of harmonics. These are called by scientists overtones, or better, upper partials. According to Zahm, " A string emitting a musical note rarely, if ever, vibrates as a whole without at the same time vibrating in segments which are aliquot parts of the whole." Violinists have found out that by touching a string very lightly with one of the fingers of the left hand, they can cause one of these aliquot parts to vibrate alone, so that we hear the upper partial alone without its fundamental. These harmonics, or flageolet tones, as the Germans call them, are used to give mystic, aërial effects, as in the closing measures of the "Lohengrin" prelude. The tremolo, a rapid alternation of up and down strokes of the bow, expresses great agitation when played by many violins not far above the middle B-flat. It is stormy and violent when given forte on the middle of the first string, and aërial and mystic in the high register.* Other

CHAP. XIII.

Special effects.

* "A Treatise on Modern Instrumentation and Orchestration," by Hector Berlioz. Other books accessible to beginners in the study of this subject are "Instrumentation," by E. Prout, in Novello, Ewer & Co.'s Series of Primers, and "The Orchestra, and How to Write for It," by F. Corder.

Muted strings.

Relations of stringed instruments.

effects in bowing are the saltato, a jumping of the bow on the strings, and the col legno, playing with the back of the bow, sometimes used in grotesque passages. Veiled and mournful sounds in slow and sustained movements or mysterious effects in quick movements are obtained by the use of sordines, or mutes, little dampers set over the strings to deaden the vibrations.

Violins are divided in the orchestra into first and second. There is no difference between a first and a second violin except in the music allotted to them. The division is made in order that the middle parts of the harmony may be properly filled out. The instruments of the string quintet may be rated as follows: first violins equal sopranos, second violins equal altos, violas equal tenors, violoncellos equal baritones, and double-basses equal basses. This is only true where all are playing together, for the viola and violoncello can go far up into the soprano register. But in the natural order of things the viola part would lie too far below the violin part if all the violins played together, so we have second violins. Modern composers often enrich their instrumentation by subdividing the first and second violins. Wagner was fond of this effect and he carried it to extremes. Violins can be divided into as many as eight parts with fine effect, but more than that are without value.

The viola is one of the most valuable members of the quintet. It is larger than the violin and its compass goes five tones lower. It is the tenor of the strings, though its music is written on the alto-clef. It is to its beautiful quality of tone that it owes its value. Gloomy, sombre, and even foreboding in the lower register, in its upper range it becomes mellow, tender, pathetic, and inexpressibly winning. No wonder that Berlioz selected it for the voice of the melancholy Childe Harold, or that Brahms made it play such important parts in his quartets. Its dramatic power is now universally recognized by composers, and from the position of a misunderstood and ignored member of the string quintet it is rapidly advancing to the equally undesirable condition of being

The viola's character.

Its dramatic power.

CHAP. XIII.

The violoncello.

Variety in the strings.

severely overworked. The violoncello and the double-bass are so familiar that it is unnecessary to say much about them. Students of scores will find that the older masters did not appreciate the expressive powers of the 'cello, as it is usually called, and seldom gave it a melody to sing. Recent composers have availed themselves of this admirable instrument, and it has become one of the most vocal members of the band. The double-bass is, of course, the fundamental bass of the entire orchestra. The string quintet, as a whole, is capable of producing a great variety of tone-color because of the large compass of the instruments. It is possible to give a melody in the soprano register to the violins, the violas, or the 'cellos, each with a different quality of tone. It is possible to write four-part harmony for violins, or violas, or 'cellos alone, and further variety can be obtained by writing in close or dispersed harmony, for few or many voices, or in high or low registers. Many compositions are written for the string quintet alone, and they are full of color.

The Orchestra

Though it is not a part of orchestral performance, but of the technics of composition, I have deferred the consideration of orchestration (the art of writing for orchestra) until now, lest in its proper place it might have distracted the reader's mind from other important matters. Let us now dismiss it briefly. The characteristics of good orchestration are solidity, balance of tone, contrast, and variety. Solidity is obtained by a proper dispersal of the harmony, so that certain tones in the chords do not stand out too prominently at the expense of others. The foundation of solidity is good writing for the strings. Their part must always be planned with great skill in harmony and a perfect knowledge of the relative tonal values of the different instruments. Balance of tone means a proper adjustment of the forces of the three choirs, so that one shall not overpower the other. In tutti passages balance of tone merges itself in solidity, and it depends partly on a proper dispersal of the harmony and partly on a knowledge of the strength of tone of each instrument. For instance, it is not

Chap. XIII.

Good orchestration.

Solidity and balance.

CHAP. XIII.

Contrast and variety.

possible to play wood as softly as strings; hence in a pianissimo, if the wood is richly scored, it will overbalance the strings, whereas in a forte all the violins in unison can drown the wood. The middle parts require to be treated with great skill. If they are too fully scored, the orchestration is thick; if not fully enough, it is thin.

Contrast is obtained by giving the melodic parts to instruments first of one kind and then of another. At one time the strings may voice the theme, at another the wood, at another the brass. Contrast is still further increased by alternating different parts of the same choir—now flutes, now oboes, now horns, now trombones. Contrast, it will be seen, also gives variety, but variety is widened by mixing tints. A flute alone has one tone; a flute with an oboe, another; a flute with a clarinet, still another. A large number of combinations is possible, and every one of them produces difference in tone-color. The music-lover should learn to note these changes in tone-color, and he should also accustom his ear to hearing the voices of all the instruments at once. A great many persons do not hear anything definitely except the principal melody, while beautiful bits of counterpoint and exquisite effects in harmony are lost to them because they have not learned how to follow the many voices of an orchestra. Every person should acquire the habit of ear-analysis. The amount of pleasure added to the hearing of a symphony by ability to hear all the instruments at once is what might be added to the delight of seeing a painting if the power to perceive the colors were given to one who had before noticed only the drawing.

Hearing all the instruments.

I have dealt as briefly as possible with the constitution of the orchestra and the characteristics of good orchestration because these topics are copiously treated in other works not beyond the reach of the general reader. We come now to the question, What constitutes good orchestral playing? This is a question which many people appear to be unable to answer, for very bad orchestral playing is frequently applauded to the echo. The requisites of good

Good orchestral playing.

orchestral playing are balance, quality and solidity of tone, precision, unanimity, flexibility, nuancing, and revelation of the value of the middle voices.

Balance of tone requires that one part of the orchestra should not overpower another. It is the result partly of good orchestration, partly of the constitution of the orchestra, and partly of the work of the conductor. The part which good orchestration plays in it has already been described. But if there are not sufficient strings in the orchestra, the brass will certainly overpower them in forte passages. With the array of brass and wood used in modern orchestras it is impossible to get a good balance with less than sixteen first violins, sixteen seconds, twelve violas, ten 'cellos, and eight double-basses. More strings can be added without damage, but with advantage, for the quality of tone will be improved because in moderato passages each individual stringed instrument will not have to be forced quite so much. The conductor's part in preserving balance is naturally to see to it that players of sonorous instruments, such as trombones, do not play too loudly.

The quality of tone should be rich, smooth, and sweet. The audience should never hear the scratching of violin bows nor the hoarse barking of overworked brass. The clarinet should not squeak, and the oboe should not wheeze. Everything should have that liquidity and mellowness which comes only from good instruments in the hands of good players. Solidity is due partly to good orchestration and partly to good playing. There can be no solidity of tone if the quality is bad or if the balance is disturbed. Lack of solidity comes sometimes from bad acoustics in a hall, and at other times from a lack of unanimity in the orchestra. Lack of it also arises from paucity of instruments. Solidity is easier to recognize than to describe, but no one can fail to detect the difference between a full, substantial, resonant body of tone and one that is thin, hollow, or nasal.

Precision means accuracy in beginning and ending a tone. The attack, as it is called, of every phrase should be so

CHAP. XIII.

Precision and unanimity.

precise that the orchestra speaks as one voice, and the end of a tone should be reached by every instrument at exactly the same instant.

Unanimity demands that all the instruments should play exactly together all the time. No one should ever precede or drag behind another. Otherwise the rhythms of the composition become clouded and the music sounds ragged. Brilliancy is out of the question when there is no precision nor unanimity. These two qualities belong to accuracy of performance and a rigid, technical accuracy is a *sine qua non* of good orchestral performance. Precision and unanimity are to be obtained only by frequent and arduous rehearsals and by the constant working together of the members of an orchestra.

Flexibility is an essential of good orchestral playing. The music should never sound rigid, but should seem to come in a sinuous stream of purling sound. Absence of flexibility is due sometimes to bad playing, but more often to bad conducting. A conductor whose temperament is phlegmatic and whose beat is rectangular will take all the flexibility out of a fine orchestra.

Nuancing means attention to the manifold nuances of light and shade. An orchestra should have a very fine pianissimo and a stunning fortissimo, and it should have every gradation between these. The conductor must see that proper attention is paid to all the crescendi and diminuendi, the hastenings and retardations of time, and the other factors in light and shade.

The revelation of the value of the inner voices is the conductor's business. He should see to it that melodic fragments, bits of counterpoint, and significant touches of all kinds allotted to instruments not engaged in playing the principal melody are sounded so that they can be heard by the audience. Composers do not write such passages with the expectation that they will be lost.

These are the essential qualities of good orchestral performance. Any person with a musical ear can recognize their presence or detect their absence. All of them should always be present in a

CHAP.
XIII.

Duties of a conductor.

good performance. The function of the conductor is partly to drill his orchestra till it possesses these qualities in its playing. His additional duty is to study and analyze each composition, form his ideas as to the proper manner of its performance, and then impart them to the orchestra. This is done at rehearsal, not at the concert. All that a conductor does in the presence of an audience is to beat time, to indicate to the various players their points of entrance, and by certain signs to remind them of what he told them at rehearsal. He and he alone is responsible for the interpretation of a work, but he does not magnetize an orchestra into following his ideas at a performance. He teaches the ideas at rehearsal, and it is there that his work is done.

XIV

Chamber Music

IN the performance of chamber music one should look for the same excellences as those of orchestral playing, with something added. Balance and quality of tone are absolutely essential to good quartet or trio playing, but, of course, it is not possible to obtain from three or four instruments that massive solidity of tone which is expected from an orchestra. On the other hand, in a string quartet there should be a perfect homogeneity of tone, an absolutely exact agreement of quality and force, which no orchestra could quite equal. This homogeneity is obtained partly from equality of excellence among the instruments, and partly from good work by the performers. If the composition be a piano quartet or trio, the piano is

Homogeneity of tone.

likely to offend by disturbing the balance of tone. There are few pianists who play chamber music well, because they are either unwilling or unable to subordinate personality to the general effect. Chamber-music organizations encourage this condition by advertising the pianist who is especially engaged for a certain work as a soloist. People fall into the habit of asking who is the soloist at a chamber-music concert, and they listen to the Schumann quintet as if it were a piano solo with string accompaniment. Some compositions justify this view, because the piano part is made so prominent, but such is not the case in the works of the great masters. A gentleman said to me after a concert: "Didn't Joseffy play the Forellen quintet beautifully?" Now, as a matter of fact, Mr. Joseffy did not even attempt to play the quintet, but kept his part in its proper proportion to the whole like a true artist. But my friend went to hear Joseffy and he did not hear anyone else. People who listen to chamber-music compositions in which a piano figures ought to remember that there is no solo in the matter, and should expect and demand of the players correct balance of tone.

Precision, unanimity, flexibility, and nuancing can all be carried to a finer finish in chamber music than in orchestral performance. Four players, inspired by devotion to their art, animated by a common sympathy which is the result of long association, and guided by deep and earnest study of the works before them, can play with a unanimity, with a finish, with a subtlety of expression which no orchestra can hope to attain. But the person who attends chamber-music performances, especially those of string quartets, must be prepared to accept, in lieu of the brilliancy, the power, the splendor of color, and the opulence of sound of an orchestra, the chaste and naked beauty of the pure music voiced by instruments whose utterance is intimate, confiding, winning, and exquisitely polished. The string quartet is never imposing and grandiose, but its art is like that of classic sculpture in its repose, its purity, and its elevation. It is the most intimate form of music, and

Taste for chamber-music.

it is heard to the very best advantage in a small room "where two or three are gathered together." To love and understand quartet playing is the surest evidence of good taste in music, because this is the form of entertainment in which the sensuous element is most kept in the background and the most direct appeal is made to the judgment. Persons who desire to arrive at a comprehension of form, and of the æsthetic qualities of music, should attend string quartet concerts frequently.

XV

The Piano

WE come now to a consideration of instrumental solo performance, and it is natural to take up piano playing first because that is the most plentiful. More people go to hear piano playing than any other form of instrumental solo playing, and this is because so many persons practise piano playing. Judging from observation extending over a tolerable number of years, I should say that out of every one thousand persons who attend piano recitals about one has any real knowledge of what constitutes good piano playing. This sweeping assertion includes all the pianists, music-teachers, and students who go on complimentary tickets, for I have witnessed a greater display of ignorance of the true significance of music as an art

Ignorance about piano playing.

CHAP. XV.

Technic and tone-color.

at a convention of musicians than at any other musical gathering I ever attended. Liszt is credited with having uttered this bit of smartness: "Three things are necessary to make a great pianist: first, technic; second, *technic;* and third, TECHNIC." And technic, in one form or another, is what the great mass of listeners to piano playing hear. The man who can strike the largest number of notes in a second is their hero, and their amazement is modified only by the sensuous delight which they get from a luscious tone-color, appropriate or inappropriate to the music. And over all floats that mysterious personal influence of the artist, which compels so many thousands of persons to listen with their eyes.

Millions of pages of black spots laid upon staves of five lines are in the world. Some of them were written by men of marvellous genius, and though they represent nothing but sequences of sounds in orderly array, the judgment of the world has accorded them fellowship with the works of Michel Angelo and Dante, which speak at once through the eye to the heart of every man who can see and read. Even the dramas of Shakespeare live in the seclusion of the library, for the printed word vitalizes the imagination, and the tragedy of "Hamlet" enacts itself within the four walls of a man's skull. But music, the one art which has no exemplar in nature, and whose printed symbols are as mystic to the man of ordinary culture as the hieroglyphs on the tombs of the Pharaohs, must wait always the mediation of the interpretative artist. Whether it be but ingenious arabesques of tones or the language of emotions too deep for words, the pathetic fact remains that in the shrine of the printed page it lies dead and entombed till the Gabriels of art sound it in the trumpet tones of its own resurrection.

It is not strange, therefore, that when the interpretative musician sits robed in the garments of high priesthood in the temple of music, the devotees should sometimes forget the gods whose administrator he is, and bend the knee of worship before him. His mission is so gracious, so beneficent, so mysterious

CHAP. XV.

Music must be heard.

Power of the interpreter.

Instrumental Performance

CHAP. XV.

Paderewski an example.

in its methods, and withal so potent in its results, that he becomes at once a teacher, a benefactor, and a ruler. Let us, for the sake of enlightenment, and that we be not swayed blindly as the devils were swayed by Orpheus, inquire wherein lies the power of a great pianist. To do so demands a review of piano playing and the deduction therefrom of certain principles to be applied as tests to the work of any particular player. I shall, I believe, not be accused of a lack of appreciation of other players if I quote, as an embodiment of these principles, Ignace Jan Paderewski, one of the greatest living pianists.

Let us look first, then, at the technical aspect of his playing, for that is what is most patent. It lies at the very gate of observation, and invites us to enter. The technics of piano playing in their lowest sense are the mechanics, the operations of the machinery of fingers, wrists, and arms. Let it be admitted at once that technics include ability to strike without error and at a given speed all the notes set down in a composition. The street-pianos, operated by turning a crank, possess the best technic of this kind, but their music is fit only for Hades. The true aim of piano technic is the production of a tone of beautiful quality and singing character under all conditions of force and speed.

Back in the pre-Mozartian period Emanuel Bach wrote: " Methinks music ought principally to move the heart, and in this no performer will succeed by merely thumping and drumming or by continual arpeggio playing. During the last few years my chief endeavor has been to play the piano-forte in spite of its deficiency in sustaining sound, as much as possible in a singing manner, and to compose for it accordingly." Every advance in the art of piano playing since Emanuel Bach's day has been made by men endeavoring to do precisely the same thing. Mozart followed the son of the great Sebastian in both theory and practice. He demanded of the pianist a smooth, gliding movement of the hands, so that the passages should flow like wine and oil. In order that the vocal character of piano music might be preserved, Mozart wrote continually

CHAP. XV.

Object of piano technic.

Emanuel Bach and Mozart.

in the cantabile style for the instrument, and constructed much of his music of passages founded on the scale. It must be borne in mind that the piano of Mozart's day was the old harpsichord, whose fleeting tones never could have lent themselves to the mass effects of later composition.

When Clementi began to write for the English piano, with its heavy strings and long hammer fall, he aimed at greater sonority than had been known before, and introduced runs in thirds, sixths, and chords. Beethoven was satisfied with Clementi's technics, and made no advance in piano playing *per se*. The mighty Ludwig was occupied with revealing the emotional possibilities of music, and it is an undeniable fact that some of his piano compositions, great, indeed, as pure music, are not characteristic of the instrument for which they were written. It remained for later musicians to show how the new percussive effects could be made amenable to the fundamental command that the piano must sing. Chopin and Liszt explored the resources of the modern instrument, and to them we owe the revelation of its possibilities in variety of tonal quality and vocal sound. The secrets of modern tone may be traced to two principal factors—perfectly equal development of all the fingers, which leads to their absolute independence, and management of the pedals.

Independence of fingers.

The supreme achievement of Mr. Paderewski's technic is its demonstration that the singing tone and perfect control of every variety of tone-color are possible in all circumstances, no matter how difficult the passage. This is the acme of technical accomplishment, and it is the explanation of the marvellous witchery of sound which the Polish pianist produces from the blows of hammers upon metal strings. There was a time when it was considered sufficient to play a rapid running passage or involved phrases smoothly, accurately, and without pounding. But that has not satisfied Mr. Paderewski. He has held the theory that the singing tone must be preserved at all hazards, and his study has been to perfect his digital facility to that end. His control of the striking force of his

The singing tone.

fingers is masterful. His employment of the different positions of fingers, wrists, and forearms is always correct, and its results are perfect. Pianists know that some teachers advocate the elevation of the back of the hand, and others its depression. Mr. Paderewski uses either position according to the tone he desires to produce. And his pedalling is simply beyond description. He seems to do almost as much playing with his feet as with his hands. And it is all for the sake of tone-color, for it is the combination of expert pedalling with the variety of touch that colors the tones.

But even the singing tone would become monotonous were there no rhythm in the playing. Rhythm in piano playing resolves itself into correct timing and accentuation. Every note must have its proper duration or the rhythm is disturbed. Every tone must be sounded with the correct dynamic relationship to those which precede it and those which follow it, or the rhythm disappears. Further than that the contours of the melodies are spoiled. The phrasing is disarranged, and the musical outline of the composition is distorted. Rhythm is, of course, primarily a matter of artistic judgment, but it is conveyed to the hearer by the blows of the fingers and is the mechanical result of absolutely just distribution of force. It is, therefore, dependent on the same technical accomplishments as tone-color. Mr. Paderewski's rhythm is flawless. He never offends the most judicious listener either in quantity or in dynamics, but, on the contrary, accentuates in such a manner that the phrasing of a composition comes out in the clearest possible light.

So much for the mechanical features of Mr. Paderewski's playing. But behind the technic is the soul of an artist. Without musical emotion that can be communicated to the hearer the most exquisite touch in the world will have no effect. Temperament—temperament—is what we all cry for. What is temperament? It is hard to define, but easy to discern. We know that Jean de Reszke radiates with it, and that Melba is absolutely without it. All we can say of it is that it is musical organization. It

CHAP. XV.

Musical temperament.

CHAP. XV.

Emotion and performance.

is the vital spark which lies in the soul of an artist to be fanned into luminous fire by the sound of his own music, so that the world may bask in the splendid glow. It is inspiration, for which poor, yearning, hungry aspiration is so often mistaken.

Mr. Paderewski has a powerful musical organization. He is, as Mr. Swinburne would phrase it, "filled full to the lips and eyes" with temperament. He throbs with emotion, which may be accepted as the threefold product of nationality, personal character, and experience. The Poles are a keenly susceptible people, and they are full of fire and passion. They have suffered much, and their emotions have become a part of their national heritage. Mr. Paderewski is a Pole, and he is one who combines the national characteristics with a gentle, amiable, and sensitive character of his own. This is not the place to speak of personal experiences which have deepened the emotional nature of this artist. It may suffice to recall the old story of the singing master who, on hearing an unimpassioned soprano, said:

"If I were that woman's teacher I would marry her and break her heart, and in two years she would be the greatest singer in Europe."

Silly stories have been told about the current of Mr. Paderewski's thoughts while at the piano, and it has even been said that he usually leaves the stage with tears coursing down his cheeks. Such talk is absurd. No one knows what are the artist's thoughts while he is playing; but it is a safe assertion that he would never have attained his present eminence if they were not absorbed in the work of his hands. The capacity to receive the emotional content of the music and the ability to transmute it through his own execution to the mind of the hearer are the results, as we have seen, of nationality, character, and experience; but the act of revealing these results must not be a mere burst of emotional impulse, for that would be destructive of all art. The emotion of the artist must be controlled. It must be under the command of the will, which in its turn must be guided by the intellect. Music is a glorious ship upon the ocean

Chap. XV.

Control of emotion.

Intellect in command.

of art; emotion is the breeze that fills the sails; intellect is the skilled hand at the wheel.

The province of the intellect in the study of music for performance is by no means difficult to determine. It is the designing power, and the design must be based upon a full and sympathetic perception of the formal and emotional beauty of the work in hand. Christiani, in his "Principles of Expression in Piano-forte Playing," allots this work to emotion, which he describes as the power of conceiving and divining the beautiful.

This, of course, is only a partial statement of the truth. The emotion of a musician contributes the sympathetic element, without which no amount of intellectual application will be sufficient to reveal the content of a composition. The player must be able to feel the composer's emotion or he cannot reproduce it for the hearer. Dr. von Bülow failed here; he showed with much skill the construction, or purely musical beauty of every work, but he could not transfer its emotion. On the other hand, emotion without complete intellectual perception results in mere sentimentalism, and is more likely to obscure than to reveal the constructive work of the composer. As Adolph Kullak says: " Mere diversity of expression does not suffice to render the interpretation beautiful. The most manifold variety in the distinctions of tone, power, and movement must bear a fitting relation to the unity of meaning of the individual composition. It is the latter which must first be recognized and understood; starting from this only, as the poetical essence, should the player calculate the proportions in which the multifarious shades are to be laid on."

The intellect, therefore, has a twofold duty. First comes the acquisition of information as to the general character and purpose of the period to which a composition belongs and the individual theories of the composer. No player, for example, is justified in reading a Mozart sonata as if it were the work of a contemporaneous composer. He is in duty bound to remember the general character of piano music in Mozart's day, and also the glorious boy's own

CHAP. XV.

Emotion and shading.

Historical justice.

Instrumental Performance

Chap. XV.

Making a reading.

Analysis of the design.

personal theories as to piano playing. The second and more serious business of the intellect is to make a keen and exhaustive analysis of the work in hand, to the end that in the reading the artistic proportions designed by the composer may be faithfully preserved. From these two operations of the intellect we get a synthetic result, which is usually termed a reading. The technical manifestations of this reading are in the general tempo, the placing of crescendi and diminuendi, of forte and piano, of hard and soft touch, of staccato and legato, or what is usually included under the vague expression, light and shade.

Variety of tone-color, contrasts of power, and all the other elements of musical expression, may be distributed in such a way as to produce a ravishing effect upon the ear without resulting in truly artistic work. It is only when the intellect has so analyzed the work that these things are correctly placed that the masterpiece glows before us in its original power, convincing us and swaying our emotions. Mr. Paderewski is a man of well-disciplined mind. He has broadened his perceptions and strengthened his reasoning powers by the study of many subjects not connected with music. His innate refinement has been polished by culture, and he has also made himself a complete master of musical construction. He analyzes a composition with the skill of a mathematician, but with the feeling of a man of powerful musical temperament. That he goes through this analytical process with the smallest works in his repertory, as well as with the largest, is abundantly demonstrated by the exquisite adjustment of his purely technical effects. Not a single measure is ever read in a slovenly manner, but each one is treated with the most loving care for its melodic outline, its individual rhythm, its rhythmic relation to the remainder of the phrase, and its office as an element in the composition as a whole. No matter how rapid or mechanically difficult the passage, the result of Mr. Paderewski's private study as revealed to his hearers is manifested in this remarkable insistence upon the artistic relations of the thousands of tones in a composition, coupled

CHAP. XV.

Adjustment of effects.

Grasp of organic unity.

with a mastery of tone-color which preserves at all times the vocal illusion. And behind all this lies a mental grasp of the organic unity of the musical work, which gives to us a symmetrical and satisfying interpretation.

In listening to the performance of a pianist the reader should apply the considerations which have been set forth. In these days complete technical equipment is not only to be expected, but demanded. The end of technic is tone, and the listener to piano playing is justified in measuring the value of the artist's technics by the range of his tone-color, or at least by the general beauty of his tone. Intellectual grasp of a composition is also to be expected of a good player, and emotional warmth is an element whose absence makes truly great performance impossible. Interesting, indeed, a purely intellectual player may be, and such a one is always worth hearing; but emotional power is what moves and melts an audience, and since there is some emotion in all music, there should be some in all playing. The cold and glittering brilliancy of a player who is

Value of emotional power.

simply able to play fast and with a glacial tone is not the acme of good piano performance, and the attendant at piano recitals should not look for the pianist's best work in those compositions which are dazzling superficialities. Bach, Beethoven, and Schumann are better tests of a player's ability than the astonishing works of Liszt. The latter composer does, indeed, reveal the technical resources of the instrument, but to play Beethoven's "Waldstein" sonata perfectly requires a great pianist, while a tolerably good one may make a surprising effect with a Liszt Hungarian rhapsody. What has been said of the beauty of music itself applies well to that of its performance. Beauty in piano playing is the result of high intellectual conception, warmed by emotional force and made known through the medium of ample technic.

Chap. XV.

Summary of the matter.

XVI
The Violin

EVERYTHING that has been said of the relations of technic, intellect, and emotion in the constitution of good piano playing applies also to solo violin performance, and, indeed, to all musical performance. It remains, therefore, only to consider the especial qualities of good technic in violin playing, and this may be done briefly. As in piano playing, the highest function of technic is the production of beautiful tone, so it is in violin playing, with the addition, which is at once a new difficulty and a large advantage, that the player wholly forms the tone himself. If you go to a piano and strike the white key just below a pair of black ones, the instrument, if in tune, will sound a true C, and no matter how you strike that key you cannot get

The violin technic.

any other note. If you put a violin under your chin, press one of the fingers of your left hand upon a string and draw a bow across that string, you may get a tone belonging to one of the scales producible from the piano and you may get one a fraction of a tone out of the scale. The violinist, in other words, must locate the pitch of each tone by the pressure of the fingers of his left hand upon the strings.

This placing of the tones has been named "stopping," the fingers being said to "stop" the strings at certain points. Accuracy in stopping is the first requisite of violin playing, because inaccuracy means playing out of tune, which is, of course, not to be tolerated. To play or sing out of tune is to make an inharmonious noise which is not music. When a violinist plays on more than one string at a time, as he does in sounding thirds or a chord, he must practise what is called double stopping, and as this is more difficult than single stopping, it belongs to the more complicated technics of the instrument.

But in addition to the accuracy of pitch

Accuracy of stopping.

CHAP.
XVI.

Quality of tone.

Touch in bowing.

in his tones, the violinist is responsible in a larger measure than the pianist for their quality. The quality of tone in violin playing is due to excellence in the instrument, to the character of the finger pressure in stopping, and most of all to the manner in which the bow is drawn, or the bowing, as it is called. The motion and pressure of the elastic violin bow are responsive to the slightest gradations in the muscular action of the arm and wrist, and as these are guided directly by the brain, it may be said that the design of the player is communicated almost directly to the instrument. Great as delicacy of touch may be in piano playing, it is far greater in violin performance, and hence every player's tone has individuality of character, and this reflects very strongly the personality of the player. It would be foreign to the purpose of this book to enter into a detailed account of the methods of tone production in violin playing. But it is proper to tell the reader what he has a right to expect from a good violinist. It has already been said that his stopping must be accurate, and this accuracy must

The Violin

be preserved in the most intricate passages. Every tone should be in tune and it should also be distinct. Many violinists blur their rapid passages, because their finger technic is so insufficiently developed that they are forced to smear the fingers uncertainly over the strings. This is an imperfection in technic, no matter how fine the violinist's work may be in other respects.

The tone should always be pure, mellow, and sonorous. It should be pure in that crystalline clarity which comes from absolute freedom from scratching of the bow or twanging of the strings. The tone ought to seem to flow spontaneously from the instrument, and the mechanical process of rubbing the bow back and forth should be like little children, seen, but not heard. The scraping of the horse-hair or the vibrating of the string should be indistinguishable. The tone should always be mellow. It should not be squeaky, or metallic, or wooden. There is a liquidity in a good violin tone, which always reminds me of the sound of running water. And the tone should always be sonorous; that is, it should be

Purity and sonority.

Instrumental Performance

Chap. XVI.

Large and small tone.

vibrant, not dead and hollow. The attentive hearer will note that some violinists have a large tone and others a small one. The difference is partly in instruments. For instance, a Stradivarius violin usually has a bigger tone than a Guarnerius. A new violin will sometimes have a bigger tone than an old one, but the latter will outshine the former in purity and mellowness. But the body of tone produced is largely due to good technics. A fine violinist will get a larger tone than a poor player from the same instrument. This difference is due almost entirely to difference in skill in bowing.

The bow arm.

The bowing is, indeed, the soul of violin playing. The bow-arm should be strong, and from shoulder to finger-tips it should be perfect in its flexibility. One of the best tests of free and flexible bowing is a sustained staccato passage. If it is played clearly, lightly, and yet firmly, the bowing is good. Passages in which several notes flow from a single stroke of the bow require much skill in the arm, while those in which each note has one whole stroke demand great freedom and power. Playing close to the bridge, where the strings do not vibrate readily, produces a nasal tone. Playing a little farther away from it gives a powerful, though sometimes harsh tone. As the bow approaches the finger-board the tone loses power and gains in mellowness. Playing over the finger-board evokes sounds very soft and much veiled. Violinists who are masters of the technics of their instrument know how to combine the different varieties of bowing with the different placing of the bow upon the strings in such a way as to obtain a wide range of effects, all of which help to make the wonderful expressiveness of the violin. Quivering of the fingers of the left hand is employed to produce a vibrato which is effective when not used too much, as it generally is. The special effects of violin playing, harmonics, saltato, pizzicato, the use of mutes, etc., have already been mentioned. All of them are, of course, employed by solo performers. All that has been said about violin playing applies to the viola and the violoncello, with the qualification that the latter

CHAP. XVI.

Violins as singers.

Intimacy of the violin.

instrument does not admit of such agility of execution, and is especially irresponsive to solo tricks in its lower strings.

Instruments of the viol family are by nature singers, and the listener should demand of solo players a constant flow of pure, vocal tone, no matter what be the nature of the music. It is no excuse for a violinist that the rapidity or complexity of a passage, causes his tone to become thin, cold, or scratchy. If he cannot preserve the pure flow of singing tone in such passages, he should play simpler music. Let me beseech the reader to set his face against mere displays of acrobatic skill in violin playing. I have, to my horror, heard a violinist of great reputation transform a Philharmonic concert into a fiddle circus with one of Ernst's show pieces. Technics should always be a means, not an end. Violinists who make cadenzas unto their own glory should not be encouraged, for virtuosity has always been a stumbling-block in the path of true art. The violin is the most intimate of all instruments. Tucked under the player's chin, and responding to every touch of his hand, it becomes a part of himself. He should never make it a mere medium for the exhibition of technical tricks, but should use his skill in stopping and bowing to make it sing.

VOCAL PERFORMANCE
XVII
The Work of a Chorus

Requirements of choral singing.

THE effective performance of vocal music is dependent so largely upon purely technical considerations that it seems wiser to consider first the work of a chorus, in which the essentials of good singing, as exemplified in the delivery of a fine soloist, are so obscured in the emission of a great volume of tone that the more readily perceptible qualities are those closely akin to the excellences of orchestral performance. As these have already been reviewed, it will be easier to mention the requirements of choral singing first, and afterward take up those of solo work. The requirements of good choral singing, then, are quality and balance of tone, correct intonation, attack, precision, unanimity, phrasing, shading, and enunciation. The reader, who has already perused the chapter on orchestral performance, will not be at a loss to understand the signification of most of these terms. In a chorus the quality of tone should be full, vibrant, and pure. It should not be a mere noise, which almost any large chorus can produce, but should always be sweet and musical, no matter how powerful it is. It should be a smooth and fluent tone, without harshness or huskiness. And there should be a volume of it commensurate with the size of the chorus. It is remarkable what a big tone some small choruses produce and what a small one proceeds from some large choruses. This is, of course, a matter of good singing on the part of the individuals who comprise the chorus.

Balance of tone is absolutely essential to good choral work. There should not be a preponderance of any one part, or of any two parts. In most choruses the tenor department is weak, because it is difficult to get competent tenor singers. But such a weakness is, of

CHAP. XVII.

Singing in tune.

Importance of phrasing.

course, a defect. The ideal balance of tone is that in which each part—soprano, contralto, tenor, and bass—is capable of precisely the same degree of power. Correct intonation is an absolute necessity in choral singing. No singing out of tune should be tolerated. The relations of the parts to one another in respect to pitch should be accurately maintained, and, furthermore, the whole body should keep the correct pitch, and not permit it to sink down half a tone or more between the beginning and the end of a number. By attack is meant the onset of the vocal force at the beginning of a passage. This should be firm, sure, and masculine. It should never be weak, timid, irregular, or uncertain. Precision and unanimity have already been explained. These terms have the same meaning when applied to choral singing as they have when applied to orchestral performance. By phrasing is meant the division of the melody into connected groups of notes, each of which groups is to be sung in a single flow of breath. The places for taking breath are the intervals between

The Work of a Chorus

the phrases. Good phrasing is an essential quality of all singing. In the work of a chorus the phrasing must be arranged by the conductor, and it should be such that neither the contour of the melody nor the sense of the text is disturbed. A single example will suffice to show what is meant. In a chorus of "The Messiah" is the following passage:

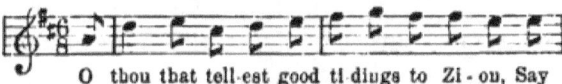
O thou that tell-est good ti-dings to Zi - on, Say

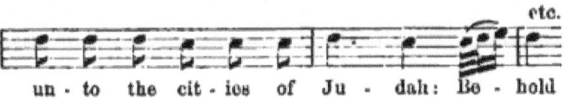
un - to the cit - ies of Ju - dah: Be - hold

It is absolutely fatal to the beauty of this passage to take breath at any points except those indicated by the punctuation. Handel fitted his music so perfectly to the text that the literary and the musical phrasing are one, and if the singers take breath at other points than those indicated they not only spoil the sense of the words, but upset the melody as well. Not every passage written for chorus is as easily phrased as this. The

CHAP. XVII.

Light and shade.

Refinement and size.

duty of the conductor is to aim at a phrasing in difficult passages which will as far as possible preserve both literary and musical sense. If he is forced to sacrifice one or the other, he must follow the composer and sacrifice the words. The musical phrasing must always be preserved.

Shading, or nuancing, has already been explained. It only remains to be said that choral singing is capable of the greatest niceties of light and shade, and these refinements should be expected. Enunciation, of course, means a clear delivery of the text. There is no reason at all why the text of a chorus should not be enunciated in such a manner that the audience can follow it. It can be done, and therefore it ought to be done. The text is intended to be heard, not to be lost in indistinct mumblings. The listener, however, must make some allowance for the size of the chorus before him. A body of say one thousand voices is likely to be somewhat unwieldy, and no conductor can get as much refinement from such a chorus as he can from one of half the size. It is the custom of musical managers to make a great noise in their advertisements of a big chorus, and such a body is, indeed, imposing in mere volume of tone; but a small and well-trained chorus of some two hundred selected voices will far excel it in quality, attack, precision, unanimity, shading, and enunciation.

XVIII

Solo Singing

Ignorance about singing.

OF all the branches of musical performance singing is that about which the great majority of music-lovers know the least. I have never heard any vocal solo so bad that there were no persons in an audience ready to demand an encore. On the contrary, very bad singing, if it is only sufficiently pretentious, arouses much enthusiasm, and the general public makes very little discrimination between the work of a De Reszke or a Melba and that of a fourth-rate Sunday-night concert-singer who has paid the manager to give her an appearance. Singing is difficult to judge calmly and dispassionately, because the personal influence of the artist, exercised almost without the intervention of a medium, reaches the hearer with a direct force; and a panting, screaming, dramatic soprano, who is really full of passion, and who projects temperament into the atmosphere as a hose would squirt water, stirs up an audience powerfully, and sends people away crying: "Oh, what a divine singer!" On the other hand, a woman who can sing trills, scales, and staccati with accuracy and rapidity may be as void of feeling as an oyster, but she will get great glory simply by amazing her auditors. Between these two extremes the finished cantilena of the cultivated vocal artist is lost, and the critic who mourns the infrequency of a polished legato style is voted an old fogey.

Singing is the most clearly expressive form of music. Song has text which makes the emotional schedule plain, and the music, following the text, is vital with feeling. The singer, using this hybrid but powerful art form and infusing into it the potency of his own temperament, sways an audience at will. It is obvious that the highest type of song is that in which the music most accurately voices the emotional content

Temperament and agility.

of the words. It is equally obvious that the highest type of singing is that which is devoted to the interpretation of this kind of song, whether it be a mere song or a whole opera. The greatest singer of the lyric stage is the most accomplished impersonator of the famous dramatic rôles, it being understood that operatic impersonation demands perfect vocal technics. The great concert-singer is one who excels in the delivery of the most artistic songs, not in that of claptrap ballads or empty show pieces like Proch's "Air and Variations."

But there are certain well-established qualities of vocal technic, and these are what the general public seem not to know. I have heard a famous contralto who strewed the stage with the *disjecta membra* of the vocal art applauded to the echo, simply because she had a big, sonorous voice. The same people went mad about Jean de Reszke, the greatest male singer of our time, the finesse of whose art was wholly beyond their perception, though they felt its influence. Now there may be a good deal of difference of opinion as to the correct interpretation of a song, but as to the technical merits of its delivery there should be none whatever. Whether a person sings well or badly is not a matter of opinion, but a matter of fact. Fortunately I am not called upon to explain the physical processes by which good vocal technic is produced. I should, indeed, be in a sorry plight were that my duty, for I know of no subject on which there is so much disagreement among professors. Every one of them appears to have a different method, and they waste much good and useful time in hurling vituperation at one another in the columns of the musical journals. I suspect that many of them have a good deal more method than is beneficial to their pupils, and I am of the opinion that my friends, Jean and Edouard de Reszke, who advocate processes in song similar to those of well-rounded speech, are nearer to the laws of Nature than many of the teachers. All that I am called upon to do in this book, however, is to direct the attention of the reader to the results aimed at by good vocal technic, to the end that he may note when

Difference of methods.

CHAP. XVIII.

Registers and equalization.

they are present in the work of a singer or absent from it. I shall not attempt to go into the extreme niceties of the art, because such an undertaking would require a volume larger than this. I invite the reader's attention to a brief outline of the fundamental principles of good singing.

The voice itself may be a great gift of Nature, as in the case of a Patti or a Melba, or it may be the result of studious cultivation of only tolerable material, as in the case of Jean de Reszke. But in either case there are several registers—I dare not say how many, because the professors do not agree on that point. But almost anyone will consent to a division of the voice into upper and lower registers. One of the fundamental requirements of a singing voice is that these registers should be equalized. This means that there should be no audible change of quality as the voice passes from one to the other. Some voices are so poorly equalized that the upper and lower registers sound like two different voices. Mr. Walter Damrosch's criticism on Melba's voice was a significant description of perfection in this essential. He said: "There are no registers at all in that voice; it is all one."

This equalization of the registers belongs to the general department of tone-production, which is the foundation of all good singing. The secret of good tone-production is management of the breath. It is the passage of a column of air from the lungs through the vocal cords which sets those cords in vibration, and these vibrations make the sound. Every sung tone ought to sound to the hearer as if it were formed just behind the teeth of the singer. It should be absolutely pure; that is, all the breath should be turned into tone and none should be allowed to escape with a hissing sound. The tone should be clear; that is, it should never sound as if there were some obstacle in the singer's mouth that prevented part of it from coming out and kept it muffled down in the throat. It should be free; that is, it should never sound as if it were sung through a squeezed-up throat, a process which produces the tone called "throaty." A

CHAP. XVIII.

Good tone-production.

Clearness and freedom.

"throaty" voice has something of the quality of the voice of a person who tries to speak while swallowing. These essentials of a good tone depend entirely on the manner of propelling the breath from the lungs through the vocal cords. Though I do not desire to enter into technics, it may not be hazardous to say that a good tone-production is largely dependent upon the attack, that is, the beginning of the tone. On this point I give way to the author of "The Philosophy of Singing," Mrs. Clara Kathleen Rogers:

Secret of attack.

"If the tone is uttered or struck at the precise moment that the breath is given up, a perfectly clear, bell-like and positive attack, as of a note struck sharply on the piano, will be the result, and the effect will be both restful and delightful. Moreover, the tone will expand, travel, and fill not only the largest auditorium, but, what is better, it will also fill the auditor." In another place the same author says: "If the meeting of the vocal cords in sound anticipates the liberation of the breath, the tone attack is hard and explosive. If, on the other hand, the liberation of the breath anticipates the closing of the vocal cords, the result is that the tone sounds as if it began with 'h.'"

A good singer should have a perfect

legato style as the foundation of his manner of delivery. "Legato" means "bound," and in a legato style the tones are bound together in a single current. Each tone is sustained until the very instant that the next one is begun, yet the voice at the conclusion of the first tone must not gradually slide through the interval between that and the next one. That effect is called "portamento," or carrying the voice. It can be used occasionally with beauty, but its constant employment is a grave defect, and leads to all kinds of bad singing, including singing out of tune, which, indeed, is not singing at all. In all pure, fluent melody, such as the themes of songs and of operatic airs, a pure legato style is a *sine qua non*. In dramatic declamation it is, of course, not so necessary, yet it underlies all good singing.

A good singer should have complete command of the *messa di voce*. This means the gradual increase of the dynamic force of a sustained tone to its fullest capacity and its diminution to the faintest pianissimo. It is upon this power that the expression of emotion

CHAP. XVIII.

The legato style.

Messa di voce.

CHAP.
XVIII.

Vocalization.

largely depends, for it enables the singer to make crescendi and diminuendi and other effects.

Pure pronunciation of the vowel sounds is an absolute essential of good singing. The artist must be able to produce a good tone on any of the vowel sounds at any musical pitch within the scope of the voice. This is one of the greatest difficulties of singing. It is technically called "vocalization." When you read in a criticism that a certain singer's vocalization was good, it means emission of vowel sounds—not singing. The processes by which the difficulties of vocalization are overcome are involved, and some singers never master them. Two singers of our time, singers of wholly different styles and purposes, are fine examples of perfection in this matter. They are Jean de Reszke and Francesco Tamagno. On the other hand, a German tenor, admired throughout Europe always vocalizes the word "Maria" at the end of the first scene of "Tannhäuser" thus: "Mari-i-oo-wuh," and people applaud him for it.

To pure emission of vowel sounds

Solo Singing

must be joined distinct enunciation of the consonants. Again I point to De Reszke and Tamagno as exponents of perfection in diction. Their articulation is so distinct that every person in the audience can follow every word of the text sung by them. There is no reason why the words of a song should not be clearly enunciated. Singers who do not enunciate clearly, simply do not know how. Mrs. Rogers, whose words voice my ideas so well that I have difficulty in avoiding absolute plagiarism in writing this chapter, says:

Distinct enunciation.

"In spite of the fact that consonants form for a brief moment an obstruction to the vocal sound—inasmuch as the sound which passes freely through the mouth in singing vowels is intercepted either wholly or in part in consonants—they never really prove a hindrance to perfect tone-production when the singer understands the nature of the different consonants and their relation to vocal sound. The singer who sacrifices clearness of sound to smoothness of vocalization labors under the great mistake of supposing that these two qualities cannot be harmonized. They not only can be harmonized, but the one can be made to help the other."

Of phrasing I have already spoken in connection with choral work. Good

Good phrasing.

Chap. XVIII.

Regulation of breathing.

Technic and art.

phrasing is an essential of artistic singing. Breath should never be inhaled at any point where the action is an interruption of the musical idea. A melody must not be broken into disjointed fragments to accommodate the breathing of a singer; the breathing must accommodate itself to the melody. It would benefit many singers to study the laws of musical form, for good phrasing must obey these laws. It is the duty of the composer to write his music in such a way that its phrases are coincident with the rhythmic phrasing of the text. But if the composer has not paid strict attention to this matter, the singer must use his judgment, and he should be guided by the musical form.

Few and apparently simple as these requirements are, they are the fundamental qualities of good singing. The overwhelming influence of such art as that of the MM. de Reszke, Mme. Patti, Mme. Lehmann, and other great dramatic singers of our time, is due to their perfect command of these technics, which they make a medium for the expression of their personality and their emotional force. Whether we are moved by the intense pathos of M. Jean de Reszke's Tristan, the majesty of M. Edouard de Reszke's Wotan, the stupendous passion of Mme. Lehmann's Isolde, or the sparkling vivacity of Mme. Patti's Rosina, we owe our delight to the perfect adaptation of their vocal powers to their purposes. The ornaments of singing, which are the stock-in-trade of the colorature singer, are surprising because they are difficult, but surprise is not the aim of true art. Mme. Patti was in her day, as a St. Petersburg writer said, "the Paganini among vocal virtuosi," but it should also be remembered that her delivery of a simple melody was the perfection of pure legato singing. There was a time when trills, staccati, and roulades were regarded as indispensable to good singing. Mancini called the trill the "support and life of song," and Tosi declared that one who could not produce a good trill could never be a great singer. The world has outgrown such ideas, and to-day we demand of an artist a pure dramatic cantilena, and care little

Mme. Patti's skill.

CHAP. XVIII.

Ultimate purpose of song.

about cadenzas. At the same time we must ask of singers who do attempt the ornamental style perfect flexibility and accuracy of execution. There are texts to which such a style is the best adapted, and whatever is done in song must be well done. Furthermore, all these ornaments are valuable as exercises in acquiring command over the vocal organs. But the high purpose of song is deep emotional expression, and for this the trills and jumps are of little value. In the domain of true vocal eloquence, pure tone, perfect legato, messa di voce, correct phrasing, and distinct enunciation are, and always will be, the reigning powers.

Index

INDEX

ACCOMPANIMENT, a tune its own, 29; of chords, 29; in song, 78
Æsthetics, of music, 117 *et seq.*; laws of, 120 *et seq.*
"Aida," 84
Analysis of a tune, 24 *et seq.*
Answer, 31, 32
Aria, origin of, 80; development of, 80 *et seq.*; kinds of, 85
Arioso, origin and nature of, 80
Art song, 76
Art-work of the future, 5
Attack, choral, 182
Augmentation, 32

BACH, EMMANUEL, 159
Bach, Sebastian, 31, 38, 39
Balance of tone, 143, 146
Bass, double, 140, 142
Bassoons, 134, 135
Beauty, defined, 117 *et seq.*; free and adherent, 118, 119; place in music, 119; man's conception, 124; abstract in music, 124
Beethoven, his romanticism, 65; sonatas and symphonies, 42; rondo form, 45; theme and variations, 55; scherzo, introduced by, 57; transitional period, 61; method of expression, 103; piano technic, 160
Bowing, 174 *et seq.*
Brahms, 69
Brass choir, 136 *et seq.*
Breath, management in singing, 191 *et seq.*
Bülow, Dr. von, 166

CADENCE, 23
Canon, laws of, 30
Cavatina, 56
'Cello, see Violoncello.
Chamber music, 151 *et seq.*; qualities of performance, 153; taste for, 154
Chant, Gregorian, 37
Chorus, work of, 180 *et seq.*
Clarinets, 134, 135
Classic, era, 60 *et seq.*; music, 61; *vs.* romantic, 63 *et seq.*
Clementi, 160
Climax in sonata, 53
Coda, 53
Concerto, 60
Conclusion, in sonata, 46, 53
Conductor, duties of, 150
Content of music, 88 *et seq.*
Contrast, of themes, 47; in orchestration, 144
Conventions of expression, 112

Index

Counterpoint, 30, 38; church, 73
Countersubject, 31, 32
Couperin, 45
Criticism, without knowledge, 3;
   vs. enjoyment, 4; basis of, 89;
   evils of bad, 111

DE RESZKE, EDOUARD, 189, 196, 197
De Reszke, Jean, 163, 188, 189, 190, 194, 195, 196, 197
Descriptive music, 113
Design, demands of, 99
Development, thematic, 50 *et seq.*
Diction in singing, 194, 195
Diminution, 32
Discussion in sonata, 46, 50
Dvořák, 58

EMOTION, ruled by intellect, 98, 165 *et seq.*; expression of, 102; and performance, 164
Emotional, the, 104 *et seq.*; æsthetics of, 123
Enunciation, choral, 184; solo, 194, 195
Episodes, 49
Equalization of registers, 190
Expression, laws of, 105; conventions of, 112
Expressive powers of music, 104; basis of, 105; limits of, 107, 109 *et seq.*; nature of, 108

FANTASIA, free, 50
Finger, independence of, 161
First movement form, 46 *et seq.*; outline of, 54

Fitness, 122
Flexibility, 148
Flutes, 134, 135
Form, need of knowing, 15; material of, 18; melodic, 22, 37; polyphonic and monophonic, 26 *et seq.*, 41; origin of, 35 *et seq.*; polyphonic, when developed, 38; romantic, 63 *et seq.*; Schumann's modifications, 66; fundamental principles of, 70 *et seq.*; vocal, 73 *et seq.*; song, 75 *et seq.*; operatic, 79 *et seq.*; the intellectual and, 101, 103; the governing principle, 125
Fugue, 31 *et seq.*
Furiant, 58

GLUCK, operatic reforms, 81
Greeks, music of, 37

HANSLICK, theory of musical beauty, 101
Harmonics, 138, 139
Harmony, nature of, 21
Haydn, 42; character of his music, 61, 62
History, musical, need of knowing, 15, 110
Horns, 136

INEVITABLENESS, 121
Instruments in orchestra, 132
Intellectual, the, 97 *et seq.*; and design, 98; in piano-playing, 165
Intonation, 182

Index

Introduction, in sonata, 47
Italian opera, weakness of, 83

KANT, on Beauty, 117
Kettle-drums, 138
Keys, relations of, in first movements, 49

LASSO, ORLANDO, 34, 38, 39
Laws, recognizable, 14
Legato, 193
Legno, col, 140
Lehmann, Lilli, 196, 197
Listener, the uninstructed, 7 *et seq.*
Liszt, 67 ; concertos, 68

MELBA, 163, 190
Melody, nature of, 21
Messa di voce, 193
Metres, musical and poetical, 25
Minuet, 56
Monophonic music, 41 *et seq.*
Moods, music expresses, 108
Motive, 23 ; repetition of, 24
Movements in sonata, first, 46 ; second, 55 ; third, 56 ; last, 59
Mozart, 42, 45 ; character of his music, 61, 62 ; operas, 81 ; piano playing, 159

NETHERLANDS SCHOOL, 34, 74
Neume notation, 35
Nuancing, 149, 184

OBOES, 134, 135

Opera, origin of, 79 ; purpose of, 82 ; requirements of, 83 ; Italian, 83 ; artistic level of, 86
Operatic forms, 79 *et seq.*
Orchestra, constitution of, 131 *et seq.*; instruments of, 132 ; the three choirs, 133 *et seq.*
Orchestration, qualities of, 143 *et seq.*
Organism, attributes of an, 100
Organization, 17, 18, 99
Overture, programme, 68

PADEREWSKI, 158 *et seq.*
Palestrina, 34, 38, 39, 74
Patti, 190, 196, 197
Pedals, 161, 162
Percussion, instruments of, 137 *et seq.*
Performance, qualities of, 129 *et seq.*; orchestral, 145 ; chamber music, 151 *et seq.*; piano, 155 *et seq.*; violin, 172 *et seq.*; choral, 180 ; solo-singing, 186
Period, 23, 42
Phrase, 23
Phrasing, in piano-playing, 162 ; choral, 182 ; solo-singing, 195
Piano-playing, 155 *et seq.*
Polyphonic music, 30 ; history of, 34 ; characteristics of, 39
Portamento, 193
Precision, 147
Programme music, 114
Programme notes, 68
Programme overture, 68
Proposition, melodic, 23 ; in sonata, 46, 49

QUARTET-PLAYING, beauties of, 153

RECITATIVE, origin of, 79; kinds of, 84
Registers of voice, 190
Repeat, in sonata, 49
Repetition, 16; distribution of, 17
Rhythm, 18; elementary, 19; simple and compound, 20; origin of, 35; in piano-playing, 162
Romanticism, 4, 63 et seq.
Romantic school, forms of, 67 et seq.; traits of, 69
Rondo, 44 et seq.
Rossini, weakness of, 83

SALTATO, 140
Scherzo, 57 et seq.
Schubert, his romanticism, 65
Schumann, symphonic form, 66
Score, place of instruments in, 132
Section, 23
Sensuous in music, 88 et seq.; elements of, 92 et seq.; laws of, 95
Sentence, musical, 23
Shading, 184
Singing, choral, requirements of, 180 et seq.; solo, 186 et seq.; true purpose of, 197, 198
Solidity in orchestra, 143
Soloist in chamber music, 152
Sonata, 46 et seq.
Sonata form, 46 et seq.; essentials of, 54; departures from, 59; Schumann's modifications in, 66
Song-forms, 75 et seq.; folk, 75; cyclical, 76; art, 76; lyric and dramatic, 77; requirements of, 78
Sordines, 140
Stanza, 42
Stopping, violin, 173
Story, telling a, 115
Stretto, 31, 32
String-choir, 138 et seq.; division of, 140
Style, suitability of, 122
Subject, greatness of, 13; in fugue, 31, 32
Symphonic poem, 67

TAMAGNO, FRANCESCO, 194, 195
Taste, readily acquired, 7
Technic, piano, 156, 158; violin, 172 et seq.
Temperament, 163
Thematic development, 50 et seq.
Themes, in sonata, 47; community of, 66
Tone, qualities of, in orchestra, 143, 146; in chamber music, 151; piano, 161; violin, 174 et seq.; in choral-singing, 181 et seq.; in solo-singing, 191 et seq.
Tone-color, 95, 161
Tone production, vocal, 191 et seq.
Touch, piano, 160 et seq.
Tremolo, 139
Trombones, 136, 137
Trumpets, 136, 137

Tschaikowsky, 58
Tuba, 136, 137
Tympani, 138

UNANIMITY, 148
Unity, organic, 99

VERDI, 84
Viola, 140, 141; playing, 177
Violin, in orchestra, 138 *et seq.*;
 first and second, 140
Violin-playing, 172

Violoncello, 140, 142; playing, 177
Vocal forms, 73 *et seq.*
Vocal performance, 180 *et seq.*
Vocalization, 194
Voices, inner, 149

WAGNER, 5, 6; operatic form, 81, 84
Wood wind, 134
Working-out, in sonata, 50; value of, 53

www.ingramcontent.com/pod-product-compliance
Lightning Source LLC
Chambersburg PA
CBHW022018220426

43663CB00007B/1130